D0518713

BLACK BOOTS & FOOTBALL PINKS

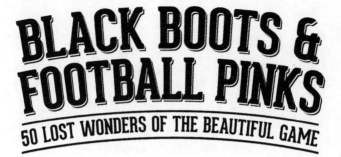

BLACK BOOTS & FOOTBALL PINKS
50 LOST WONDERS OF THE BEAUTIFUL GAME

DANIEL GRAY

BLOOMSBURY SPORT
LONDON • OXFORD • NEW YORK • NEW DELHI • SYDNEY

BLOOMSBURY SPORT
Bloomsbury Publishing Plc
50 Bedford Square, London, WC1B 3DP, UK

BLOOMSBURY, BLOOMSBURY SPORT and the Diana logo are
trademarks of Bloomsbury Publishing Plc

First published in Great Britain in 2018

A catalogue record for this book is available from the British Library

Library of Congress Cataloguing-in-Publication data has been applied for

ISBN: HB: 9781472958860; ePub: 9781472958877

2 4 6 8 10 9 7 5 3 1

Typeset in Haarlemmer MT by Deanta Global Publishing Services,
Chennai, India
Printed and bound in the UK by CPI Group (UK) Ltd, Croydon
CR0 4YY

MIX
Paper from
responsible sources
FSC® C020471

To find out more about our authors and books visit
www.bloomsbury.com and sign up for our newsletters

To the girl I lift when we score.

CONTENTS

Preface: Or, sketching the ghosts before
    they leave the room   xi

1. Multiple cup replays   1
2. Spontaneous atmosphere   4
3. Proper division names   7
4. Black boots   9
5. Ramshackle dugouts   13
6. Disorganised warm-ups   17
7. Knowing the names of grounds   20
8. Goalkeepers in trousers and hats   23
9. Local shirt and hoarding sponsors   26
10. Football Pinks   29
11. Queuing for tickets   33
12. Big man/little man up front   36

CONTENTS

13. Player jobs after retirement 39
14. Matches played in fog 42
15. Shirt etiquette 44
16. Kids playing in the street 46
17. Checks, tartans and other turf patterns 50
18. Small men marking the post 53
19. Old-fashioned wingers 55
20. Sharing the scores from elsewhere 58
21. Ceefax and Teletext 61
22. Terrible goal kicks and foul throws 64
23. Club season-highlight videos 67
24. Abandoned matches 70
25. Home away, home away 74
26. Referee occupations and hometowns 76
27. Players running onto the pitch 79
28. Loan moves being rare 82
29. Choosing who you're next to 85
30. Main-stand clocks 88
31. One-club men 90
32. Beams and imperfect views 93
33. Sponsored players' cars 96
34. Homes with views into the ground 98
35. Turnstile operators 101
36. Shabby training grounds 104
37. Characterful captains' armbands 107

38.	Provincial businessman owners	109
39.	Caretaker managers	112
40.	Paper tickets	115
41.	Player brawls	118
42.	Pixelated scoreboards	121
43.	Huts on stand roofs	125
44.	Regional highlights programmes	128
45.	Luxury, superfluous players	131
46.	Bald players	134
47.	Goal nets with personality	136
48.	The many scents of matchday	139
49.	Understated goal celebrations	142
50.	Heroes	144

Acknowledgements   146

PREFACE

OR, SKETCHING THE GHOSTS BEFORE THEY LEAVE THE ROOM

Thirty years ago, I went to a football match for the first time. The environment of those early supporting days shaped my obsession. Here was a sport closer to its Victorian rise than its televised future.

Over these three decades, much of what I knew has faded away or been replaced. It has been both a fascinating and a heartbreaking time to be in love with football. I am marked by a desire to record what is gone, the consequence of which is this book. I wish to preserve in words the relics of our identity.

My supporting life has straddled two worlds – 'old' and 'new' football. I am guilty of glorifying the former and tutting at the latter. Right or wrong, I know I am not alone. This book is for those people who look at a picture of, say, Maine Road and sigh with longing. It is for people who miss being told the hometown of a referee, and pine for miserable turnstile operators or pixelated scoreboards. I hope that it will make some of these things feel within touching distance, even if that can never again be so.

I have written it, too, as my own subjective record for people who don't miss those days, or weren't there. Whatever your outlook, this is an account of what some of us saw before all memory of it fades. It is an attempt to sketch a ghost before it leaves the room. In some ways it is written from the future. Not every wonder is gone from everywhere – not every last turnstile operator has yet been replaced by a scanner – but it soon will be. That is the course set for the game, unless authorities and financiers start to value preservation and authenticity as many supporters do.

Each piece that follows is unashamedly nostalgic and sentimental. Such qualities are often scorned, as if to be pro-nostalgia is to be anti-progress and against all change. Yet there is nothing regressive or conservative about looking back when it brings solace and joy or provides an escape from the everyday. There may even be ideas here worth resuscitating. I saw the unifying powers of recall with my earlier book, *Saturday, 3pm*, whose more nostalgic chapters often provoked a warm, amused and even buoyant reaction.

There is a danger here, of course, of revisionism. December 1988 in Middlesbrough was four months before April 1989 in Sheffield. I recognise that old football was not some sprightly Maytime – there are no entries on the thankfully departed, from fences to casuals. Where old scents of football are remembered, they are of the Bovril rather than bodily type.

I have tried not to rant or moan, though on occasion that proved impossible; pointing out what *is* becomes necessary to contextualise what *was*. It is important, too, to recognise what corporate money and globalisation have taken from the game. Millions of us feel alienated, feel the game has lost much of its personality, and that so much character has been thrown away.

Here then is a last goodbye, a celebration of what we had. There is, as I hope I have shown before, much to delight in about the modern game. This glimpse backwards, though, seeks to offer cosy refuge from a boisterous game and world. Come back with me.

1

MULTIPLE CUP REPLAYS

There can never be too much football. For some of us, it is there to block out things we struggle to understand. The longer we can keep the curtains drawn, the better. League games, domestic cup games, European games, summer tournaments. Even, in desperation, pre-season friendlies. Play on, give us excess of it. If anything, there should be more of it, cheering and speeding up our weekdays too – imagine how much faster an afternoon would shunt along if there were scores to check up on or radio commentaries. We do not have to be there; it is just reassuring to know that football is going on.

When penalty shoot-outs toppled the limitless cup replay, we lost one such caterer to our excessive needs. An eternal fountain was stemmed, sealed and left to decay. No more winter nights of two teams inseparable, clutched together in a rigid deadlock through a dozen kick-offs and six equalising goals. Such an impromptu string of games was the nearest football got to a Test match series. On day one, a scoreless draw meaning a Wednesday night 2–2, and that after extra-time. Then, another 120-minute impasse, and a further replay.

When the stand-off was at last settled by one team's slender victory, it seemed both a shock and faintly bad-mannered. The players were now familiar with one another. There was mutual respect among persistent equals – perhaps friendships across the halfway line bloomed. Supporters knew opposition players as well as they knew their own. They were on nodding terms with away-end stewards. Both managers had run out of tactical insight or game plans, and relied only on prising yet more effort from their charges and the hope of a fluke goal. Interminable replays bred a grudging form of solidarity.

There was much to admire in just how thoroughly equal the two teams were. In its own way, the repetitious cup tie was like watching two boxing greats jousting for hours on end. Again and again, these two teams cancelled one another out. Each attacking manoeuvre was met by a mirror defensive reaction. Everything was null and void, with each occasional goal struck dead by a leveller. It was either the height of sporting contest, or a symptom of goal-scoring ineptitude. Probably both.

By the third or fourth game, replay footballers were clobbered by a seismic breed of tiredness. Everything hurt, inside and out. On pitches of clumpy grass and sinewy mud, they had run pointless marathons with no finish line. Then, after seven or nine hours of slog, a saggy, weary, clumsy, drooping, floppy goal would end it all. Two hitherto disparate clubs now had an infamous period in common, a holiday romance beneath floodlights.

2

SPONTANEOUS ATMOSPHERE

On that divine and hopeful strut to the match, there were the sounds you passed and those you went towards. Drifting by the mouthy callers selling programmes, lotto tickets and burgers, and the soloists and choristers intoxicated by ale and nerves singing their hymns in an unknown key, your ears guided you ever forwards to a fixed target. The football ground was speaking to you. Its muffled din of announcements and tinny records summoned and beckoned.

Walking these streets that on Saturdays were surely yours, it could be heard beneath everything. It was an entirely pleasant form of tinnitus, a comforting sound lining your ear. It was faint background noise, as pleasant as birdsong or a milkman's whistling. It intruded upon nothing, and seemed barely louder inside the ground than outside. The announcer's voice was smothered. Though the player names read out in the line-ups were familiar, it took effort and strain to decipher them, as if someone was whispering at you through a gas mask. There may then have been run-out music, but it was easily overcome by throttling applause and furtive chants. Then the supporters were left to it. They made their own noise.

There was no juggernaut sound system vibrating the sky, no pre-match bombast. Atmosphere was spontaneous, impulsive. There was no hint of a choreographed *experience* or *spectacle*, no ear-smashing dance anthems raging right up until the referee's whistle, no cacophonous announcer telling you to 'make some noise'. Merely, a few thousand people singing and cajoling in those bullish and utopian minutes prior to kick-off.

That went for scoring a goal, too. Scoring is a fundamental of why we bother. Everything is about scoring. Everything leads there and everything results from the act. When the ball goes into the net there comes over us a bliss and forgetfulness quite impossible to find elsewhere. It is the reward for our sufference, our money spent and the justification for our obsession. In the seconds after a goal is scored there is euphoria both personal and communal – first, our own unbridled, abandoned joy; then, a second wave of noise and arms around the person next to us. These days though, in some high turret an announcer is already cueing up after-goal music as leather hits string. When the game finishes, he kills your roars, boos and elated or heartbroken chatter with news of club-shop opening hours and ticket details, quickly followed by the residues of his tired music collection. It is like being in a conversation throughout which somebody goes out of their way to talk over you.

To think that in those better days, standing and listening to the matchday hubbub gave you the same cosy feeling as being in bed, listening to a gale ruffling the roof tiles.

PROPER DIVISION NAMES

For a century, all was simple. The laws of mathematics, and not marketing, were obeyed. Even when there was a slight deviation, it had the effect of adding richness and clarity; there is something grounded about 'Third Division North' and 'Third Division South', something reassuringly factual. It feels more of a clarification than a change. Now, a division is frequently called a league, and the fourth tier is named 'two'.

Classification and rank have value in football. Supporters wallow happily in this snobbery. The relegation of a rival club is not just a sporting setback, it is a humiliation as they are cut adrift, demoted to some wilderness or afterlife. 'Down to League One', though, does not have the same degree of doom and aspersion as did 'Down to the Third Division'. It is softer, a mild rebuke where once we had in our vocal arsenal a reserve of piquant tirade. Falling to The Championship sounds like a compensation, where a lapse into the Second Division reclassified you and very distinctly announced that you were now of a lower set.

The rebranding of divisions has removed an edge, made proceedings less enjoyably cruel. No longer is that rival feathered and tarred. There is, too, a softening of feeling in gaining promotion – so much less drama and depth in rising from Championship to Premier League, rather than the giant leap from second world to first.

Renaming has blurred what was sure and plucked confusion from what was a clear hierarchy. Each time changes are made, they leave us feeling like some baffled postman attempting a round in a street where house numbers have become letters of the alphabet. Explaining to an outsider which division your team plays in ends up as an apology for confusion caused, as if, with diving players and bloated salaries, it is another of football's transgressions for which you are somehow partly responsible.

4

BLACK BOOTS

After a while, most of it passes you by. Where once the apparatus of football were noticed and often cherished, now they are overlooked. New kits are impossible to become excited about and appear to be merely recycled versions of old ones. It is announced that a supersonic ball, lighter than a grape, will be deployed in the forthcoming season, but all you can think about is the simple industrial pragmatism of the Mitre Delta 1000. The season starts with a fad – snoods, nasal strips, Vaseline on shirt chests. It seems so very finicky when you lived through a time of full-backs strangling their ankles with gaffer tape.

In those days of fixating upon such things, of *caring* about a new shirt's collar shape, it is possible that *you* played eleven-a-side too. Indulging in such full-blooded weekend mornings meant knowing a second tier of paraphernalia. Shin pads mattered, even if their squelchy ankle guards and cumbersome foamy entrails swelled lower legs to bollard size. A boot bag, its zip forever becoming caught on a lace from within, became a required accessory. There were accoutrements that seemed to appear from some monochrome age, a rope linking a father's generation to his child's: Dubbin; stud keys; boxes of spare studs; and needle adaptors for inflating balls.

Acquiring such furnishings meant ceremony, not least in the buying of boots. There you would stand before a wall of studded shoes, each given a small shelf so that they appeared to float as do objects in the strange rain of a surrealist painting. Some, though unobtainable in the budget set by a parent, you would pluck down and caress, as if desire alone might goad a lunge into wild spending excess.

With a more likely purchase identified, and a shoebox's rustling promise unleashed, came the time to trial the boots and check whether they could harness a season's growth. Big-toe test passed, it was a happy young person who left a shop with new football boots in a carrier bag. Parent and cub were lost in a moment of tender commerce. One could look back and feel happy that the spirit of a child once fixated with Lego and colouring-in lived on; the other was unknowingly sparkling with the final fragments of untainted youth.

Those boots – now to be worn in through blisters that turned every floor into hot coals, then clacked together and cleaned on the backdoor step – were, of course, black. Always black.

It has taken the recent trend towards neon boots to make me care a little about a matter of style and gear; brightly coloured football shoes have released in me an entirely curmudgeonly, possibly snobbish, form of nostalgia. Boots should not be candy-floss pink nor the sickly turquoise of toothpaste. They should not be warning-sign red nor the silver of a miserly sky or the yellow of chips in curry sauce. There is nothing classy about these shades. The feet within them should be allowed to sing without the aid of such deafening microphones. The artistry of football is in human toes, not sponsored trimmings and marketing pseudo-science. Coloured boots make me want to leap over the hoardings and two-foot their wearers. Naturally, I will be wearing black boots should I do so.

Black boots are down to earth. They say 'collectivism' and 'solidarity' where coloured boots are individualist, often worn by those who think themselves to be superior players. Black is sure, it is honest eye contact and a wink back to early footballers trampling around in their factory boots. It is substance and solidity. To see a black boot now gives the glow of spotting a vintage bus.

5

RAMSHACKLE DUGOUTS

What heavy thoughts must have trudged across the mind of a football manager leaning on a ramshackle dugout. Seldom did he strike that pose when things were going well. While all around him was noise and pandemonium, he stood among the fog of a thick silence. He was there and not there, lonely in a gathering of many. His mind talked loudly and madly of substitutions, tactical changes and what to say to the press.

Not all weeks were like this. On some afternoons, the dugout made him feel like an emperor looking across the Coliseum. He sat loosely and wrote confidently on a notepad, was able to command routine nods from his assistants and coaches. He stood and barked instructions as if he truly believed that football matches could be controlled.

Alongside him in the bunker through storms and sunshine was a regular cast. Those assistant managers and coaches, ready to enact his wishes and daring to leak thoughts of their own. A twitchy physiotherapist, alert as a fox in an aviary, medical holdall at his feet. Substitutes, waiting for a part to play, muscles warmed and stretched soft.

For a supporter, watching the movements and interactions of the benched crew and the manager was a dazzling sideshow, a bonus concert. An old dugout – widely lost now to secretive uPVC and heated car seats – offered open-air, visible theatre. It presented one small way in which the spectator had advantage over those inside the game. There they stood like pantomime villains with their backs to the heckling thousands, their view worse than that of a mole surfacing for air. A main stand loomed intimidatingly over a dugout like a cruise liner over a dinghy.

What splendid and eccentric dugout specimens there were. As sculptures of homely DIY prowess they crouched on each side of the tunnel like sunken sentry boxes, bulwarks against mob rule. Most were shaped like squat, open-fronted sheds or bus shelters, staunchly quadrilateral and blocky. On one fascia, a painted sign marked 'Home', on the other 'Away', or the exceedingly polite 'Visitors'. Signage daubed other surfaces too – advertisements or hopeful pleas for 'No Swearing'.

Rickety dugouts were apparently crafted from the spoils of local builders' yards. Everything was used inventively and lovingly in the tradition of shiplap village halls and Perspex garden lean-tos. Where there is roof felt, there is affection, and the infectious enthusiasm of a hobbyist.

Some were made from corrugated iron, further enhancing the protective air-raid shelter ambiance of a dugout. Elsewhere, timber and steel were deployed, or bricks, often painted in team colours and reinvigorated by July's ritual sprucing-up of the ground. The use of breeze blocks created an unusually understated form of Brutalism, as did internal concrete floors and paving slabs laid in front, a kerbed patio leading to a spacious and bumpy lawn. For seating, planks of wood suspended on bricks, or the same fold-down seats that supporters used. The ramshackle dugout was nothing if not democratic.

Oh for those charming days when a manager could accidentally bang his head on a dugout roof, and we could all feel better about ourselves.

6

DISORGANISED WARM-UPS

It was a more chaotic kind of sport. There are some elements of that game which happily have been left behind, not least those afternoons and evenings when supporters were brutally kettled and caged. Yet in creating a Year Zero and a game reborn, much spontaneous charm was managed, restructured or financed out of existence. A rapscallion, droll uncle sobered up, lost his foibles and mislaid his wild tales.

Strongly does this burn in the shift from disorganised, lawless pre-match warm-up routines to the draconian, cone-steeplechases we have today. The anarchy of the windmill stretch has been replaced by the tyranny of the wrist monitor and so many little generals in polyester.

Early arrival at the ground gifted the supporter a view upon happy mayhem. In each half of the pitch, players seemed to be doing their own thing, lost inside their imaginations like children in the school playground. Where a child makes up a game, or becomes a spaceman, the player would dart suddenly in one direction for no more than 15 or 20 feet.

Around him, all were indulged in similar acts of personal activity, some frenetic, some dawdling. Each man was idling away the last half-hour until kick-off, loitering until they had a purpose. Some stood in groups of three or four, absent-mindedly passing or heading a ball to one another. Others spluttered through various lacklustre stretches. On a pitch during any pre-match warm-up, one could see the aforementioned windmill, or a cross-legged grasp of calves, or ex-teammates from either club chatting on the halfway line while performing lethargic side lunges. Some balanced on one leg and pulled the other up behind themselves at the knee, like a swollen and pale flamingo. Over at the penalty area, a tubby coach leathered in crosses for the goalkeeper to catch, or players lashed forth shots aimed at him but destined to bounce around terrace steps.

The players then drifted off the pitch in fits and starts, those playground children reluctantly obeying the killjoy bell. At five to three they would re-emerge, pouring from the tunnel at great speed, pelting footballs into the air, running in all directions like some faulty firework. There began a secondary, shorter phase of the disorganised warm-up.

More balls were slung at the goalkeeper, while full-backs and wingers practised passing in a straight line to one another. The keeper dived and grasped to obtain a reassuring feel of the ball, a vicar comforted by his favourite bible. A couple of players practised keepy-uppies, that most enjoyable and pointless of afflictions, while others contented themselves with further sprint bursts, skips and knee-high jogging manoeuvres. The captain snarled orders of threat and encouragement, picking out individuals for hand-clapped gee-ups.

Then, a whistle commanded each man into his rigid position. Legs were shaken, some hopped and sprung up and down, and very soon the next act of the circus could begin.

7

KNOWING THE NAMES OF GROUNDS

Perhaps you could name them all. The grounds of the English 92, or the Scottish 38. Each team name induced an immediate and emphatic response: Hull City? Boothferry Park. Rotherham United? Millmoor. Falkirk? Brockville. It was word association, learnt instinct, conditioning. Yet it was also perfectly natural for the football supporter, in a way that reeling off multiplication tables never was. These were the lyrics of our lives.

Awareness of such names gave the ennobling feeling of knowledge, but also a comforting sense that your world was solid, sure and labelled. You did not have to know each and every Lane, Park and Street to lay beneath this warm blanket; just enough to feel attached and included. Feeling that everything was in its place, that everything was routine and fixed, was of universal solace.

It all bound you to neglected, faraway pockets and cubbyholes of Great Britain. You knew nothing of Stoke, but knew Stoke City played at the Victoria Ground; Sunderland *was* Roker Park. Now, The Dell is gone, The Baseball Ground too. Ayresome Park has fallen, The Vetch Field is dearly departed, The County Ground has passed on, Maine Road has been razed, Love Street is wasted, Highbury has expired, it is curtains for Gay Meadow, Belle Vue is crushed, Highfield Road flattened and Firs Park wrecked. Remnants have sometimes survived – housing-estate names, a turnstile retained outside a dreary supermarket – but the connection, and the *fact*, has died.

The ground name gave you something to identify a place by, something those unpossessed by football did not have. It honed a geographical knowledge of provincial England, Scotland or Wales which bemused others. If you met someone from Colchester or Montrose, you at least had a reference point, even if they did not like football. Further, an original name's suffixes possessed depth and the simple, evocative detail of an Usborne map illustration: road, field, park, street, lane, parade, court, moor, bank, mill, hall or crescent.

All of this is impossible with a venue named after a sponsoring airline or online-gambling company, whether a new stadium or a rebranded old ground. Many change their title every couple of years, a financed identity crisis. The reeling-off of names, the coupling of team and ground, has faded away. No longer do we know all the lyrics.

Still, if those old names were once there in your mind, they probably still are now. Using them in defiance of ground moves and sponsorship is a minor but satisfying act of rebellion; two Vs calmly raised to the slayers of Gay Meadow, Belle Vue and all.

8

GOALKEEPERS IN TROUSERS AND HATS

Winter seems to trickle in. Leaves rot to crimson dust and an air vent opens in the sky. An hour is gained and yet tea is eaten in the dark. Morning's consolation is a frost laminating the pavements and lawns, and chimney breath on the way to school. The big coats are out to stay.

It is in this weather that the football season truly begins. It has not settled until you have walked to a ground underneath a charcoal sky. It is not fully composed until you have watched a match while feeling the special kind of cold that exists at football, one undefinable by meteorologists. All is not in order until you have spent part of a Saturday afternoon shielding your eyes from the low sunshine.

At this time of year, that sun dangles, a lustrous pendulum. It hovers until half-time, then seems to curtsy and exit upon command of the referee's whistle. By then it has performed its duty of nuisance, adding extra fibre and artifice to the game. For the team with the sun at its back, this means hurtling forward high balls and spinning tall corners into the box. For the opposition, any kind of clearance will suffice – in seeps the 'if in doubt, kick it out' mantra of Sunday-morning games. Their goalkeeper, bothered by the similarly blinded heckling terrace behind him, paws at the ball, a cat grasping at string. The punch is his only asset; time and again, he rises and strains to box, thump, wallop and pound the ball.

The scene is old, a classic. Inexplicable modernity has robbed it, though, of one prop: the goalkeeper's baseball cap. Sometimes such hats have rested by the goalpost, memorials to times and custodians gone by. More often, the keeper's cap has disappeared altogether, a mystery only partly explained by confusing rules, high stadium walls and vanity.

Lost to us now is the sight of a keeper clumsily altering his hat while wearing gloves. Lost to us is how incongruous headgear looked among 21 hatless players, and just how small a keeper's head seemed beneath a cap. These were jumble-sale caps, incoherent with all other playing kit and liable to make a goalkeeper resemble a teacher dressed for a school trip. There lingered, too, the very slim and yet tantalising slapstick possibility of a goalkeeper throwing his hat down having conceded a goal.

Gone too are goalkeeping trousers. No more seen is the padded legging of yore, that protector against primitive plastic surfaces and frost-bitten pitches. The street-corner look of tracky bottoms wedged into socks is not seen, scruffy ballerina chic is no longer in. This is part of a wider erosion of goalkeeping attire and tradition. First they came for the green jerseys, then the No.1 status. Next it was mysterious kitbags thrown down into a goal as keepers ran on, and then the ritual hanging of a bar towel in the side netting. Rarely does a goalkeeper butt his studs on the posts. No longer is he the only player allowed to accessorise.

Hats and trousers were something remarked upon, something noticed. There was even an attitude that a keeper was something of a Fancy Dan, should he dress up in this manner. It played, too, on the reputation of goalkeepers as non-conformists. Now, so many have become sinewy machines like their outfield teammates – athletes, even. More's the pity.

9

LOCAL SHIRT AND HOARDING SPONSORS

There it was, that umbilical link between place and team, announced in a rampage of different typefaces. On shirt and hoarding, it spoke of a club laced into the fabric of its surroundings and conjured images of stout local businessmen with leather chequebook holders and bad suits.

Behind the goals, solid trades were advertised. Builders' merchants, tile and carpet centres, glazers and joiners. A town's respectable clan of professionals had their spots too: solicitors, insurers and estate agents. There were shops, businesses known only to those dwelling within a few square miles – the town hotel, family jewellers and a supermarket as yet unbought by a chain. There, in black block capitals on orange, kindly white fonts on blue and in friendly green italics upon yellow, was a town's commercial and industrial character defined.

Shirts told specific stories and spoke more loudly than hoardings in a world of few television highlights. The glimpse of a top at a game or in a newspaper or magazine came to be the visual representation of a place, and therefore a club's sponsor inherited added importance. To those of us whose eyes tinted everything with the colours of football, certain brands *became* a team and place once they were sponsor for long enough: Southampton was Draper Tools, Oxford was Unipart, Coventry was Peugeot, Charlton was Woolwich and Brighton was Nobo.

Now to look back at football shirts of a certain vintage is to glimpse a world of full, prospering high streets and bulky Yellow Pages. There are those sponsored by greengrocers or butchers denoted only by surnames which, presumably, were bywords for trust and quality, and in themselves have robust echoes: Braithwaite & Miller, Godwin's or GH Swain & Sons. A town's newspaper, that lighthouse beaming out local pride and In Court listings, makes a frequent appearance, harking back to the years when pages paid. There are mechanics and car dealerships, local breweries and foodstuffs, and sponsors reflecting regional industries sometimes known elsewhere – Findus for Grimsby Town, Freeman's catalogues for Bradford City.

The shirts themselves were made not by multinational manufacturers but through homespun labels whose names evoke the local sports shop: Spall, Ellgreen, Matchwinner, Influence, Scoreline, Ribero and Frontrunner. It added to the sense that each place was different, *exotic*, even. Names that meant nothing in the place where you lived but formed part of someone else's universe, and they felt the same about yours.

10

FOOTBALL PINKS

You heard him before you saw him. The evening sports paper man. 'Spoooorts Gazette' came the throaty offer in my part of the world; yours, perhaps, was another of the elongated hollers pestering the land in advertisement of Pink Finals and Green 'Uns, Sporting Stars, Arguses and Mercuries, Football Posts and Echoes.

He was a single-story town crier, his fluorescent jacket standing in for velvet robes. On corners in town and shuffling through pubs, he would push pink, green or white pages. They shrieked news of LATE DRAMA or HOME ANGUISH. Some copies hung over his arm, some rested in a paperboy's tatty bag, ready to be plucked and flogged.

Or your paper was taken from a till pile, still warm from the printing press. A van would speed up to the newsagent's, halt suddenly and its driver burst in with batches of papers, a kind of merry hold-up in reverse. Thrown to the counter, plastic twine could be liberated with scissors, and a growing queue sated, their questions of 'Pink in yet?' and 'Argus arrived?' dramatically answered. On an away day, another town's version could be snaffled from a railway-station stall, its contents both alien and familiar.

It was an astonishing accomplishment: a detailed, printed record of a match starting at 3p.m. could be read in the windy streets by teatime. In those hours a reporter had rumbled away in the ground, phoned in tidings of near-misses and dubious penalties, and whole pages had been set and checked at the newspaper office, and then printed and distributed. To think that, for the reader, the joy had only just begun...

First, there was a bracing front page to examine and consider. Its brief, bold capitalised headlines could bring drama to a spiritless 0–0 (DEADLOCK, or SHUT-OUT). When those dispatches conveyed a victory or defeat for your team (REDS DELIGHT, or

HOME DESPAIR) it granted the scoreline deserved weight. The result mattered and those capital letters agreed. The headline was accompanied by an image from that day's match. This too seemed impossible, wondrous. To behold so soon pictures of the game you had just attended … it felt as though a captured winger could skin an opponent full-back all over again, even when still, or the roar of a goal be heard in print.

Then, a flip to pages two and three for the forensic match report. A full read would come later; a first glance meant eyes jogging between capitalised player surnames, and paragraph headings such as 'Headed chance' and 'Late surge'. To see this little more than an hour after the final whistle, before the last player had signed the last autograph of the evening, seemed like an act of illusion or a bending of time itself.

Inside the paper, there was yet more fresh news of nets rippling and managers under the cosh. Late into pages six or seven, the pinks and greens of multi-team cities thronged with match reports. A win for your side and a defeat for local rivals made this newspaper an inky, fleeting fairy tale.

In that first half-hour of inhaling, perhaps the grandest treat was the majesty of the back page. All those minuted goals and scorers in faraway towns, that high crowd at Barnsley, the new league tables freshly pressed. Orderly bulletins from the other side of the border and from non-league football too. What a feat of engineering. How could all of this be possible? How could so few pence bring so much joy and intrigue? All those plotlines, knitted together and set out in calm symmetry; raw, breaking news that made you feel cosy rather than alarmed.

Football Pinks were a comfort blanket, a fixed and sure gift. They extended matchday and cheered or consoled any evening. They were weekly telegrams from the frontline of war bearing the words: 'Safe and well, home soon.'

11

QUEUING FOR TICKETS

In town, a rumour would spread that some supporters were camping out. They had pitched a tent by the ticket office, looped ropes around bollards and steel crash barriers to secure it. Such sacrifices were being made in the name of a great cause. On flasks of tea and tuna sandwiches smothered by cling film they survived. In the pursuit of a cup-final ticket, all such actions were worthwhile.

Ever since that closing whistle was sounded in the semi-final, getting a ticket had been an obsession for thousands. There was a simple, blood-curdling dread about not being there on final day, like some dream in which you forget to attend your wedding. Failing to obtain a ticket would be catastrophic and would haunt you for years. It was possible to picture another, ticketless you, walking around your empty town, all the world behind a door and you locked out.

So there you stood in a queue. It began at ticket office hatches or doors and ended somewhere by another stand. Being at the end made you a board-game counter freshly fallen to the bottom tip of some snakes-and-ladders serpent. Right now, the distant front was the flickering lights of a faraway port. In-between, this nervous column in their patchy uniform of club-coloured scarves and hats waited and intermittently shuffled forwards. All movements were furtive, inches not feet, every person a pall bearer. It was hardly worth removing hands from pockets or unfolding arms. Yet each tiny advance twinkled with hope. As the hours collapsed and you watched the sky alter in tones, it became possible to believe that a ticket would be yours.

A camaraderie between each link of the chain was probable. Even those queuing alone were united with others by their pursuit of this same prize, banded together by hopping up and down to locate some kind of warmth. There was time for chatter, most of it about your team and the match for which this eager line existed. There were contemplative silences too, each queue member lost in thoughts of where they would like to sit, and the quiet privilege of being outside a football ground on a non-matchday, of seeing how it breathed without you.

After such calm anxiety, the moment thundered in. On tip-toes could you count that there were only 26 ahead of you, then 15 … 7 … 2 … You were in, it was dizzying. There was a pile of tickets, someone serving you, a conversation, money handed over, a ticket grabbed, everything hazy. You had it, this unusually-sized piece of paper with its hallmark and its beautiful details citing the date and exact kick-off time of destiny, and the block, row and seat from which you'd watch the best day of your life unfold. Outside, you stuffed it into wallet or pocket, before some wicked and cackling wind could seize it. Remaining queuers looked at you as a dog looks up from beneath the dinner table.

12

BIG MAN/LITTLE MAN UP FRONT

He won the flicks-ons, and his partner tried to make goals happen.

He was the big man up front. There was no standard height for the big man up front, merely something above six feet. It was not as if he had set out to be the big man up front, had spent playtimes suspended upside down from the scaffold climbing frame in an effort to stretch himself longer, or had rejoiced in perfectly executing backwards-headers with a tennis ball. It just seemed to happen to some centre-forwards. A title bestowed, an inherited role, a necessary mantel. Most teams had one, so he became yours.

The big man up front could, it was said, hang in the air. This gave him a spectral mystique, or the quiet enigma of a conjurer's assistant. It made him sound wispy, ethereal, even if in reality he wore cycling shorts to protect wizened hamstrings and his neck jarred in 17 places every time he landed. Though shunting in the style of a gammy hen, the big man was adept at sudden runs backwards towards the centre-circle to pointlessly flick-on goal kicks. The big man bothered both centre-halves, narked them as a baby brother narks his older sister. Either frequently ended matches with split-lip or eyebrow-stitch. He was often a journeyman pro who had contributed 11 or 12 goals per season to eight or nine clubs, the life of the battered and roaming trouper. At each new club, supporters would take to this soldier of fortune and sing for him.

His sidekick added the guile, grew petals on the stem. Arcing around centre-halves with the hope of winning those flick-ons, or taking the ball into his feet from the big man holding up play, the little man made supporters feel as though something was about to happen. When he neared the penalty area with the ball, there was an added crackle in the air, as if sparklers were being lit. On the terraces they roared and up from their main-stand seats they stood. He scored more goals than the big man, slotted home penalties, but would also drift wide to curve knowing crosses onto his partner's forehead. He could find that cranium without looking, a pigeon flying home in the dark.

The little man was not asked to defend at set-pieces like the big man. His job was to wait on the halfway line while the industrialists toiled to liberate his artisan finesse. His head was chest-height with both his sidekick and the centre-half marking him. Two of his running steps were worth one of theirs, and yet so dainty was his scurry that he easily outpaced all. He had been the all-rounder at school, the athletics champion and the county cricketer. Come 5.30p.m., it was his autograph supporters queued longest for.

The big man/little man combination brought chances and goals, near-misses and delirium. To see them embracing after a goal like some mismatched couple who had forgotten to bring their lemonade crate was a thing of splendour, a panting sculpture. The battering ram cleared the way, the nifty knight swept in and rescued the maiden. It was a simple tactic, a crude tool, and a beautifully logical way to play football.

13

PLAYER JOBS AFTER RETIREMENT

'He used to play for Leeds or someone,' an auntie would vaguely and teasingly remark, pointing across the street at a traffic warden. 'John summat's his name ... or is it Dave?'

In her circles of the town, they did not see a fallen star of Elland Road, Valley Parade or wherever it was. They saw a man in his early 60s dispensing parking tickets, a man somebody's lad had said was a footballer.

That somebody's lad felt like you did. They felt that you could see it in his gait as he moved down the street, half-pecking at car windows, that there was a slight crumple to his knee movements. Were he small, it would be surmised that a faint limp was the price of being a brisk winger in those days of double-edged tackles.

You kept watching, transfixed by his mundane routine. Was it you, or did ex-footballers have a certain aura about them? He still looked after himself, that was clear: the slight tan both from being outside all day and treating himself and his wife – still glamorous – to a fortnight in Benalmádena; hair wax applied methodically and in a style that considered *Charles Buchan's Football Monthly* a mirror.

Did he think of those days as he helped a delivery-lorry driver reverse into the Woolworth's loading bay? As he patrolled the town-hall car park, did he have sudden flashbacks of looking up from the centre-circle at the floodlights on a European night, or long internal reminiscences of matches and goals on a projector in his head, everything in chrome-filtered colours? In the rumbling traffic could he hear the guttural roaring of a crowd?

Perhaps you looked at him as you looked at a pensioner still haunted by the mention of war, trying to imagine what he thought and what he had seen. It was nothing but awe: here was a man who had done what so many of us dreamed we would do.

Once playing careers had finished, a chosen few retirees lingered in the game, grasping what little work it offered. Most became civilians again, though never quite like the rest of us. Some ex-footballers had savings enough to have their name above the door or in the classified pages – the pub landlord, the newsagent, the sports-shop owner, the tradesman and the bookie. There was more intrigue, though, in tittle-tattle of a footballer working for someone else – the delivery driver, policeman, council maintenance man or travelling sales manager, perhaps flogging his wares across towns whose grounds he once lit up.

Occasionally, it was possible, if you had the nerve, to step into another dimension and actually speak to an ex-footballer. They were part of real life now. Many, you suspected, had been through a saddening and bewildering time of readjustment. One week they're singing your name, the next you're on the bins. That riches have spared many current ex-players such turmoil is a happy thing; the shame is that there is now little chance of ordering a quarter of Kola Kubes from a man who scored at Wembley.

14

MATCHES PLAYED IN FOG

Football has its trigger words and phrases. When heard, they spark within us a small campfire. They warm us and strike up a glint in the weariest eye. Floodlights, last-minute winner, turnstile, favourite player, terrace, away win, autograph book, league ladders, first game, orange ball... When one such term is used, those present dash off in a reverie all of their own, daydreaming of *their* first game, and the time *they* saw an orange ball used.

That orange ball seems to have a nostalgic category all of its own. Despite seldom being seen – and it is entirely possible that we only convince ourselves we have witnessed one in use – this candescent sphere clings tight to our imaginations. It rouses thoughts of a sport carrying on regardless; the stiff upper lip of football equipment. It represents, too, a departure from the normal, a special emergency, a siren proclaiming novelty. Most of all, it evokes a match played in fog.

When a match played in fog is recalled, the mind conjures a ground like something from Charles Dickens' London on the opening page of *Bleak House*. There is indeed fog everywhere. Fog up the tunnel, where it flows among teams running out. Fog on the halfway line and fog creeping into the penalty area. Fog lying out on the left-wing and hovering in the goal. Fog drooping on the beams of the main stand, and fog in the eyes and throats of supporters.

Though time and memory may thicken the haze, there is some truth in such recall. Fog *did* make it hard to see far beyond the halfway line, with players a sudden flash of darting colour like dots on the back of an eyelid. Attempting to watch the game was an act of stoicism underpinned by the surreal, football played in the clouds to the chagrin of Clough and God. A match, with its plotting and toing and froing, was unfolding beneath a veil as if the stage manager had forgotten to raise the curtain. It could be that only sound from an unseen corner would alert you to a goal. Anything could be happening. The pea-souper turned football into a dream.

15

SHIRT ETIQUETTE

Those fibres matter to us. When a supporter wears a football shirt outside of matchday, its threads wind their way invisibly back to the ground, like umbilical cotton.

Shirt colours strike something within. Supporting a team that plays in blue means a simple adherence to other items coloured the same. Blue, or red, or black and white are your primary colours. They tint your glasses and paint your favourite skies. Even as we grow older and stop wearing replica shirts, this identifier carries emotional weight.

Such a mental bond was forged in times of sure and simple shirt etiquette. Every team started with players marked 1 to 11. It was possible to know a footballer's position by his shirt number. That number was the equivalent of wearing a job title on his back. It formed one of the soothing symmetries and routines of watching a match, and made football feel more universal and equal. Some footballers came to be associated with a number, as if it were branded onto them with a hot iron poker. That '5' or '7' or '10' was as much a part of a lofty idol as his fierce tackle or mesmeric footwork.

Further protocol made for a more endearing spectacle. Away shirts were worn appropriately, not as a sales technique or under corporate duress. They were a club's 'change' colours, pulled from the wicker hamper in response to a clash with home jerseys. Under such uncommon use, they helped fix a supporter and perhaps even a team into a visitors' state of mind, ratcheting up away-end din, and binding tighter a rearguard action from their side. There were distinct conventions around the tucking-in of shirts, too: the tightly bound organising midfielder and the unsprung maverick winger. No shirt was mired in clutter – sleeve and collar sponsors, player names – just minimalist adornments, a sky free from clouds. And, what finer etiquette can there be than an unspoken agreement that mud must find its way onto shirts, the sign of a well-worked shift.

16

KIDS PLAYING IN THE STREET

It was a tender symphony of the tarmac. First you heard the thuds, strafing the air in a miscellany of notes: a scuttling sound, meaning a pass delivered at pace across the ground; ever-decreasing pauses between the ball's bounce, a street Morse code for 'wayward shot'; a slapping noise, like an oar dropped in a lake, signifying a shot on goal with laces through the ball. Then, the unmistakable thwack of that ball hitting the side of a car, the sea lapping a boat hull.

This divine instrumental was not all that could be heard. In accompaniment were carefree hollers and outraged howls, desperate pleas to receive a pass, cries of 'foul!' and 'handball!' and ecstatic cheers when a goal was scored. In that moment, nothing else mattered to both ragtag teams in their kits of scuffed trainers, jeans or tracksuit bottoms, T-shirts and jumpers. On suburban street and in village cul-de-sac, players were lost within a primitive, wild and exultant version of football. If you heard it but were not involved, it was a call to prayer.

With street furniture their props, they were shaping chronicles and writing scripts with their feet. Some pronounced them through self-commentaries. Street lamps became floodlights and leylandii were transformed into swaying crowds. The kerb was another defender to beat, the grit bin perfect for a slick one-two. It was possible to make a goal from almost anything: those same bushes and lampposts, a panel of fencing or a gate, a chalked garage wall, some handily placed hydrangea, a fire-hydrant stone and a street sign, discarded or liberated traffic cones or drainpipes. The street player was creative, an impromptu architect. When he declared that 'here' to 'there' was a goal, it became just that, a territory marked and a rule applied and instinctively understood by all who showed up to kick and dream. Finding a willing goalkeeper, however, was another matter.

These same surroundings would slow the game too. A volley could easily spiral over a garden fence, requiring a polite knock at the door or a swift foot-up and a heave over the barricade. Or it could become jammed in a tree, meaning the hurling upwards of any nearby missile, from tennis ball to breeze block. Worst of all, the ball would become lodged underneath a parked car, meaning use of the crab football position to dislodge it with feet: hack, prod, hack. Nearly, nearly, then free at last.

There were other perils – a ball punctured by a rosebush, a grazed and gritty kneecap, a greenhouse shattered, a hanging basket cudgelled like a piñata. No provoked and irate neighbour could stop a game for long, though. After all, there was no kick-off time and games had no fixed duration; you did not have to wait long for another match to begin. This kind of football was played on a loop. Neither did it stop with the dreaded appearance of a parent, a ghost in the fog beckoning you, the star centre-forward, in for tea or, worse still, bedtime. The game would rumble on through sausage and chips and still be there afterwards; the real horror was hearing that tarmac symphony behind the curtains as you laid in bed. That felt as if you were being buried alive.

Though the footballs used sometimes burst at the seams to reveal a bulbous orange gut, and the hard streets made for berserk bounces, what goals we scored. What mazy dribbles we executed and half-volleys we bulldozed into the goal. Through headers and volleys, rush goalies, Wembley Doubles and 17-a-sides, we were stars beneath the street lights, and the next goal was always the winner.

17

CHECKS, TARTANS AND OTHER TURF PATTERNS

In June and July, they created. Across the land, dogged and steady groundsmen heaved cumbersome lawnmowers up and down and side to side. Their iron beasts chugged, wheezed and belched. Air usually tinted with fried food and tobacco was now infused with noxious diesel and the sweet strains of newly cut grass.

Each year, some etched a new pattern into the turf, some refreshed their habitual, hallmark design. This was, for them, the highlight of the football season. Finished, the groundsman could look upon his virginal field and the art he had crafted and feel as a child does when opening the curtains and seeing a street cloaked in snow. For now, dastardly players and dismal winters had yet to happen. Humans and seasons were obeying the groundsman's 'Keep Off The Grass' sign, itself retouched and polished.

There was no reason beyond aesthetics for a club's pitch to be cut in a particular pattern. While football grounds themselves were so endearingly irregular and inconsistent, turf patterns brought symmetry and order. It was like putting a chandelier in a barn.

At Filbert Street and Villa Park, ribbons of grass intersected to make perfect checks, earthy lumberjack-shirt grids of artful precision. Hallowed Burnden Park was chequered too, its own squares prouder and broader, a verdant chessboard. With varied stripe widths weaved into the turf, the Goldstone Ground became an emerald tartan, while regal Anfield was an impeccable gingham lawn.

Genteel Feethams was sheared in long lines of varying width and shade so that it resembled a sprawling barcode. At Saltergate, some order beneath the crooked spire – half-a-dozen broad deckchair stripes. The Goodison Park carpet gave the appearance of a colossal solitaire board. Brisbane Road was similar, though its dots smaller and less consistent, as if a giant had dropped a Shreddie and its motif had left an imprint in the playing surface. The

Manor Ground was a Magic Eye puzzle, Springfield Park stocky prison bars, Craven Cottage matchstick streaks, and Bloomfield Road honeycomb specks.

These infinite wordsearch grids and picket-fence symmetries all spoke of an era when nothing took too much time, or was beyond budget. Care was taken, proud hyper-gardeners allowed to demonstrate their artisan craft among these working-class stately gardens. There was, in the game, more room for idiosyncrasies such as turf patterns, pitch cambers and kicking downhill in the second half. Such grass carvings were an outpouring of a more characterful and less homogenous version of football.

Back in the groundsman's world, winter gathered with all its spiteful and damaging elements. Rain and studs were a dagger through the canvas. Pitches were worn through the centre and came to look like army camouflage. Goalmouths and centre circles suffered the most, countless invasions leaving patches the shade of instant coffee. Turf patterns were lost to the mud and splutter of a long season. Only summer's next visit and the chug of a lawnmower could bring renewal.

18

SMALL MEN MARKING THE POST

The referee hoisted his arm crane-like and so the small man jogged. His head was down. There was no need to look where he was going. He was homing back to the goalpost, just as he had for five or six previous corners. From none of those kicks had he touched the ball, no toe-poked clearance or canny header over. That much reinforced the pointlessness of his endeavour, and possibly of marking the post at all. There he was a lonesome bystander. Pitched within the gaping goal frame, he seemed to shrink further, a freak-show attraction.

Each defensive player had their station, though most revolved around a moving, breathing fellow footballer. The small man had only a cylinder of metal. Perhaps it is why he remained zealously active as the corner taker prepared for the kick, springing up and down or gripping the post with emphatic force. That he was invisible to the taker added to his tragic air of fruitlessness.

In the perfect scenario, ball would be swung in and buffeted clear by a teammate. Then could the small man pitter-patter away from his post and up field. His dread was something else altogether: a bullet header, thumping shot or vicious in-swinging kick hurtling towards him. When he laid awake at night, all he could see was a pitiful pogo towards the ball, and it sailing humiliatingly over him, or, worse still, cannoning off his head and into the roof of the net.

Here was an uncomplicated tactical detail that was easily replicable in school game and Sunday league. That it was both pointless and mildly cruel somehow added to its appeal.

19

OLD-FASHIONED WINGERS

We remember the fires he lit but never the cold hours. Being a winger could be a lonely pursuit. It was not all shaking left-backs until they were hypnotised, or leaving right-backs cross-eyed. Stretches of games were spent astray from teammates, an exiled player bound to the touchline as if it were a chalky manacle. At goal kicks, the winger would stand with one forlorn arm in the air, pleading for the ball like a forgotten child at the back of a classroom. Perhaps that isolation and melancholy was part of his appeal – the winger as a tortured artist.

There was to be no cutting in-field or dropping backwards to cover a marauding full-back. A winger's place was the outermost reach of the pitch. He was stationed there, assigned to the far corner of an empire until needed in action. It seems almost decadent: a player as a resting wizard, awaiting the call for his artistry, the fact that he would be unemployed for whole segments of a game acknowledged and accepted. The winger was, to an extent, an excess and a luxury.

To see that winger in full flow, however, no matter how sporadically, explained why his blameless stagnation was tolerated, and why supporters so cherished him. In appearance, the wide man was never that, nor tall. He was often slight, though robust with it; perfect qualities for a life of twisting between defenders and being the subject of their savage attentions. Once found by his own full-back with a ball steered down the line, or galloping to a centre-midfielder's ranging pass, he became a sight to behold. It could be as perfect and captivating as watching a breathtaking act of nature, like swallows flying south for the winter. As he glided past, seated supporters rose in order as if in an impromptu Mexican wave, or manoeuvred by a magnet on his back.

With head down, the winger would torture those in his way through a mix of cunning and pace, dropping a shoulder to skip by or tapping the ball onwards and bolting beyond them. In his armoury, most famously, was the dribble, but the winger had other brushes with which to paint too – not least, the nutmeg. The nutmeg was his impudent, cherished and ornamental tool. It was an act of rebellion and a splash of art. It awakened the humdrum match and embroidered the turf with glitter. It was a status symbol flaunted, and a Molotov cocktail hurled boldly through the eye of a needle. Here was a spontaneous act of disobedience. The crowd seldom saw it coming, the defender was in a different time zone. He was flummoxed and befuddled, a toddler lost in a supermarket. The nutmegger had twisted him and turned the pitch hazy.

By whatever scheme a winger humiliated his man, the space was now his. A cross could be hung, a byline found and the ball pulled back at pace, or a corner easily won against the ricochet legs of a reinforcement defender. If his virtuosity led to a goal, a whole match's chilly quarantine was swiftly forgotten by all.

20

SHARING THE SCORES FROM ELSEWHERE

We have a need to know the scores from elsewhere. Our focus should be on our own team, on the match we're watching, and yet tidings from other grounds prick our ears. It is as if football supporters have in common with teenagers that unsettling sense that something better is happening at another party.

Or perhaps we find comfort in the idea that so many thousands of others are going through what we are. There is a strange kind of unity contained within the information that Preston North End are winning at Sunderland. Finding out the scores is, too, another peg of matchday routine, another slate that makes the roof over our heads.

What once were letters of the alphabet printed in matchday programmes and displayed on pitch-side hoardings became lines recited over a spluttering public-address system. Half-time progress reports from Fratton Park and Anfield and full-time declarations from Layer Road and Ibrox. One town's goals relayed to the gathered citizens of another. It was shared, supporters united in cheering their rival's thumping. Such egalitarianism – everyone finding out the scores at the same time, everyone getting to feel simultaneously smug or depressed – even lasted into the introduction of jumbotron screens in stadium corners.

Present were a scattering of people with radios too. During an end-of-season tie that mattered for reasons of life, death and promotion, those with radios became suddenly powerful, kingpins dishing out scores, the people forever starting the games of Chinese whispers. From their radios came the vibrations which led to pockets of ebullient cheers or desperate last-ditch yowls of encouragement. These ripples could cause alarm, but at least the ground was alive with possibility and exhilaration. Proceedings were spontaneous, electric, even if rumoured scores turned out to be incorrect, and our panics wasted.

There was a purity and sense of the communal about alphabet boards, public-address systems, big screens and radios. Finding out the score on a mobile phone is the antithesis of this. It is cold, individualist, even if the phone user then shares obscure scorelines because they affect his accumulator bet.

Going to football should represent a disconnection with the real world, a sense of being out of reach. If we are needed, then the PA man can ask us to 'report to the nearest steward'. Not only does the mobile kill intrigue; it compromises our escape from the everyday.

When light fades and the final whistle blows, those scorelines should rain down from the speakers we share. They should be taken in on an instinctive level, in the heat of the moment. Everything shared, just as football was intended.

21

CEEFAX AND TELETEXT

A stout lady was selling dreams. The plucking from an old biscuit tin of a raffle ticket, pink or blue, would mean access to a bounty. Among the prizes displayed on a boarded-off pool table were tartan slippers, lavender bath pearls and a bottle of Malibu.

She waddled between tables, a mobile Russian doll, and finally reached ours. A pound coin bought a strip, filleted by the doll with panache and slapped down in front of me. And there it was, among my five chances: ticket 302. I cheered impulsively.

Those three numbers in that order felt as warmly familiar as the phone number of a childhood home. It had taken a raffle ticket to demonstrate that they were etched on my brain and singed in my heart. The way in which unrelated events can swirl the warm breeze of nostalgia like this is a fine and nourishing offshoot of growing older as a football supporter, the past a tap on the shoulder from an old friend.

Ceefax page 302 was a constant of my youth. For many years, I saw it several times a day; there was a reason that the '3' digit on our remote control was fading faster than its colleagues. I could touch-type those numbers, dab them without looking away from page 100 on the screen. They were as integral to my day as my parents and chips.

Ceefax and Teletext seem, now, to have come from a more patient time. Those black screens with palettes of police-siren blue, dove white and rubber duck yellow, and their gobbet paragraphs, were the opposite of rolling, incessant news and analysis. Their steady poise deserved the deployment of a remote's mute button so that they might be revered in full.

Through the week, there was a routine to my use. First, to 302, and a cheerless check for Middlesbrough news, before trickling through other stories. Then, 312, 'News in Brief', a sumptuous bazaar of wantaway strikers, Achilles' tendon strains and returns to training after lengthy lay-offs. Next, to 390, 'Local Sport', to become annoyed at the repeated (and perhaps imagined) prominence of stories about neighbouring clubs, before a switch to ITV, and Teletext page 140.

My Teletext ritual matched the Ceefax trawl, with 149 playing 312. There was one added lure: blinking, dazzling adverts for premium-rate football phone lines tantalising supporters with claims of a 'Shock Move' or a 'Record Bid'.

On a weekend, these dark pages fizzled. First came team news, with injured body parts bracketed following a player's name: 'Missing for the Bantams is Ian Ormandroyd (Calf)'. From 3p.m., despite sporadic action the scores pages became impossible to look away from, each of us a bird spotter staring for hours in case of a sighting. Occasionally, the screen blinked and lifted its eyelids to reveal a goal. In town centres, some gathered outside television-rental shops to gawp at those same pages. There, as at home, they waited for pages to turn and show their team's progress, hearts pumping beneath dead-eye stares.

By teatime, 302 and 140 had translated many matches into one-page reports, collated full-time scores and updated league tables. After a win, this portal in the corner of the living room was the best thing on television that night.

22

TERRIBLE GOAL KICKS AND FOUL THROWS

The goalkeeper, lonely as a melting snowman, places down the ball. He plants it in the outer corner of his area where one painted white line meets another. Dropping his head so that chin rests on chest, he chisels three times with his kicking foot. His intention is to mine a cleft beneath the ball, helping him scoop it forwards.

He takes four or five steps backwards towards a hostile terrace of V-signs, and as he limbers up they begin their war cry of 'Ohhhhh...'. When he strikes the ball, their mantra reaches a crescendo of 'You're shit aaaahhhh...'. It is not the most eloquent of football chants, if it can be called that, but there is, sadly for him, some truth in it.

His goal kick struggles to reach the centre circle, or worse still, flings out of play for a throw-in. In his head, he welted the ball; in reality, he prodded it like a toddler forking salad. Next time, he may feign a hobble and suffer the somehow preferable indignity of an outfield player taking it for him.

The goalkeeper was never alone in his moments of rank incompetence. Foibles and mishaps were scattered across the pitch. There seemed to be no pretence of straining for perfection; no mechanical athletes programmed for working to a system or a coaching philosophy. There was risk and incompetence.

The result was some of the more fallible moments that enriched a match: foul throws which allowed supporters to feel technically and morally superior to full-backs; defensive clearances that sailed over stand roofs into neighbouring gardens; calamitous own goals from intended back passes; penalty-area scrambles in which the ball cannoned from shin to head to thigh before culminating in a glaring miss; and set-piece kick-offs where the ball was skewed straight over the touchline.

Such defective episodes made for a game easier to relate to, and unleashed that pleasant delusional indulgence of the supporter – the thought that 'I could do better than that'.

23

CLUB SEASON-HIGHLIGHT VIDEOS

Out of the unit or down from the shelf. A plastic treasure box, 20cm by 12cm. Within it, a ribbon reel of familiar tales happy, sad and indifferent. The box clacks and clicks upon opening, the VHS cassette within shudders as if caught by surprise. It is clasped and lifted towards a video recorder, then shoved in its mouth. The recorder swallows, though not without complaint; there are enough mechanical wheezes to wake the household.

You press rewind, because you want this story to begin in sunny fairy-tale August when nothing can go wrong, and the tape makes a whirring retreat. It hits the buffers with a snap, signalling time to hit Play and go to that nearby land a few seasons ago. There are some dullard scrolls of copyright screens and 'Also Availables' to forward through, lines moving down the screen like waves of barbed wire. A club badge appears above the video's title, beckoning a hasty stabbing of the Play button. Over a soundtrack of saxophone and keyboard drumbeats, and accompanied by sharp clips of slide tackles, goal celebrations and handball appeals, a voice announces that you will soon be seeing, 'All the games, all the goals, home and away'. These words are your 'Once upon a time'.

With the music still going nowhere in particular, that narrator enthuses about players 'coming in' and 'going out' for £375,000 and £120,000. Then, the first few fixtures are displayed and recalled, and the yarn can unravel. In under an hour-and-a-half, you will watch an entire season. Nine months of your life, 36 weeks of elation, being underwhelmed and frequently distraught, distilled. What a marvel.

The club season-highlight video was a story at first full of intrigue and surprise, and later profound familiarity. A maiden watch was often the first time you had seen a particular game's goals, saves and dismissals, or an away ground long known only in your imagination. Then, repeated viewings meant that the video, over reality, was the way you remembered a match and even a season. It was possible to join in with the commentary, so often had you heard it. The voices you aped varied – national television commentators, their local equivalents or video specialists. Just as motley were the videos themselves. There were highly polished *Official Video Series of the Football League* in tidily designed sleeves, and there were homespun concoctions filmed from a stand roof by one man and his tripod.

For the completist collector, these items were a joy to curate. Placed spine outwards in unit or on shelf, each season's label could be seen. 1987/88, 1989/90, 1990/91... Here among cumbersome plastic and magnetic tape were the stories of our lives.

24

ABANDONED MATCHES

All through Thursday and Friday, rain, proper rain. It settles in, becomes routine. No sign of feathery drizzle, no dry spells of relief. Rain is an accompaniment, a backdrop painted onto every scene. The sky is near and aluminium. It is like living in a lightbulb smeared with grease. The torrent can be heard donking off tiles and incessantly tapping on the shed roof.

On Friday evening, a still heavier deluge splats to earth. Normal humans fret about leaks and floods; the football supporter worries that tomorrow's match may be called off. It is the same with snow and ice. Where others rejoice at now twinkling parklands and sugary trees, or bleat about the car not starting, snow and ice are grave hazards to the fan.

Even in these times we inhabit do such fears remain. No inflatable pitch cover can vanquish our irrationality, rid us from the fear of an empty afternoon. Fewer matches are postponed now, though, and only an impossible few abandoned in action.

At 2p.m. on one such lost afternoon, later abandonment was far from a supporter's mind. The referee had stomped on crispy turf or bowled a matchball to the corner flag, and then proclaimed the pitch fit for engagement. There was no need for our clocks to stop and for empty hours to be frittered indoors. We had a joyous reprieve. It was as if we'd found something thought lost.

Conditions – conditions our bolshy game had beaten, for it was stronger than the sky – glossed the walk to the ground in wild shades. We skidded along towards a match venue that today was a hotchpotch winter palace, or waded among puddles which had turned the players' car park into a congress of rockpools. Icicles drooped from the main stand's guttering.

It seemed hardly possible that the fixture was going ahead. It made for a kind of contraband glee, as if we were doing something forbidden or in secret.

The turnstile was pushed furtively in the manner of a shy child ringing the STOP bell on a bus. We were almost checking if it was real, pushing our hands through the ghost.

Kick-off came and it was clear that this was an altered sport. In the stand, we were watching from behind clouds of our own breath or with the feeling that our blood had been replaced by rainwater. On the pitch, players strived to do their jobs like suddenly blind craftsmen. They stumbled and slithered, or stroked passes that rolled for three yards and came to a standstill in the quagmire. On an icy pitch a slide tackle meant agony, and on a sodden version a protracted lunge with muddy spray splattering all around. Incredibly, these ice skaters in shorts and jogging fish were capable of mining shots and even goals.

Such goals were not to stand, would never appear in a record book nor become a personal statistic. They would be wiped, forgotten, blanked endeavours, erased moments of glory. Abandonment saw to that. It was often preceded by another onslaught from above. Snow, a storm, fog. Sobbing clouds that just could not hold it in. Those wet passes hardly moved an inch, or a goalkeeper smashed his elbow on the petrified grass. The referee called the players off the field, or perhaps waited until half-time. Then, an announcement, delivered with all the trepidation of a messenger convinced bullets were coming his way: today's game has been abandoned. Our purpose has been removed.

There would come a few minutes of standing around, not quite in disbelief, for we had seen today's circus, but perhaps because we thought the referee would change his mind. Soon we drifted away, talk of rescheduled dates and valid tickets sheltering us from the weather. The fixture we had just seen half of no longer existed, and yet it was one we would long remember.

25

HOME AWAY, HOME AWAY

There was poetry in the rhythm. Home away, home away, home away. It soothed like the clickety-clack clickety-clack of an old train carriage, or dove coos on a promising morning. Repeated aloud, it had the hypnotic clout of some meditative chant.

The tone in which each of the two words were pronounced could be telling: 'home' a warm, rising and prolonged salute; 'away' sharp, serious and portentous. On a fixture list, home ties were lifted from the page in bold, away ties stood back with their shoulders hunched in regular type. This symmetry, a duet performed 20 times over, made for a pleasing striped pattern in print, a never-ending sandwich. Home was shouted, away whispered, the large and small bars of a xylophone.

To know that every second Saturday you would be in the ground you knew and loved best was enormously comforting. It blended with a football supporter's need for routine and ritual, complementing pre-match routes to the ground, lucky garments and always standing in the same place. Home away, home away, home away... a sweet and orderly hymn.

26

REFEREE OCCUPATIONS AND HOMETOWNS

There they were, in broadcast commentaries, those garnishing details. 'Your referee today is Mr Martin Bellamy, a school teacher from Weston-super-Mare.' 'Today's man in the middle is Mr Rodger Elliot, a financial adviser hailing from Wrexham.'

Matchday programmes were more forthcoming. Alongside team line-ups, a whole paragraph could be devoted to John Butterworth, 'an insurance clerk from Hove in Sussex. John lives with his wife and two daughters, and in his spare time enjoys fishing and Western films.' Television captions had no such spacious luxury, only flickering at us with the alluring words 'Paul Salt (Birkenhead)'.

Scrutiny of referee occupations exposed one unsurprising trend: authoritarian career choices.

Policemen, teachers, tax inspectors and traffic wardens matched the psychological profile of a referee. Monday-to-Friday vocations did not sate their need to wag a finger or issue a warning. Besides, the Saturday uniform was a study in perfection for a man with disciplinarian tendencies.

It is impossible to picture these bank managers and ex-soldiers from Southport and Lincoln without tying them and their era to that uniform. Imagine them, knocking off on a Friday night, a carbonara in the town Italian with 'the wife', and then home to fold black cloth and polyester into a HEAD duffel bag, whistle and spare in the side pocket.

This breed of referee was fittingly pernickety. Adjudicating was to him a civil service, honoured and garlanded by rules and procedures. The floppy collar of a referee's shirt was something of a mayoral chain.

Referees' places of residence offered pleasing intrigue too. They dwelled usually in small towns, conurbations without major football clubs. Was refereeing an alternative to playing in these places? Referee towns scarcely made the news nor were home to the famous. It is easy to imagine our men having near-celebrity status on the local high street, and being stopped to regale locals with tales of booking Erik Thorstvedt.

That the town was even mentioned is interesting too; perhaps it was supposed to explain something. Taken together, it is possible that the citing of occupation and place were, in some way, an apology or a mitigating circumstance for the performance about to unfold.

27

PLAYERS RUNNING ONTO THE PITCH

From megaphones above, run-out music choked to life. Its tinkling notes were a kindly siren, encouraging those outside the ground to run, as do church bells to a tardy vicar. Here was a happy, serene kind of panic.

Musical choices were eccentric and varied across the land; no shared anthems, purloined by a stadium DJ from a club elsewhere, or decreed by a central sponsorship agreement. It was not unusual to hear instrumental tunes, whether classical or plucked from a television show. Such pieces belonged to a team. Listening to them in civilian life through the week gave a sweet, somehow patriotic warmth. They belonged to you.

When the music played, the seated were risen. Its opening bars pulled them upwards as if the headmaster had entered a classroom. They stood to attention, suddenly focused. In standing areas, arms were hoisted aloft to allow room for applause. Declarations of love were bellowed over the music, an easy accomplishment in these afternoons before piercing PA systems.

Eyes from all enclosures became planted on the players' tunnel. Those in the main stand looked down from above. Behind the goals, they strained on tiptoes and stared across. Opposite, they goggled the panorama but fixated on small lines of 11 men, emerging like ants from a vent. Steered over the threshold by captains, the teams scurried onto the pitch. In many grounds, the 11s entered separately; elsewhere in unison. Their columns split, decidedly filing towards their own ends of the pitch like splashing water hitting a boulder. Some players hacked footballs high into the air, others ended their run with a climbing jump and imaginary header. Carrying the matchball as if it were some live and rare specimen, the referee trickled on last with his linesmen.

The velocity of the players' entrance onto the field stoked atmosphere. It stated their intentions. Games seemed to start more quickly when teams emerged from a burrow at pace. With no choreographed stroll onwards, and no procession of conciliatory handshaking, teams were adversaries from the start, sent to their corners to prepare for battle.

The type of tunnel helped – usually a cavern hollowed into the main stand, with no snaking rubber barricade in sight. This aperture had tall sides, so that a player was spurred by bullring adrenalin rather than cuddled onto the pitch. For an away player, it meant intimidation, too; intimidation that fuelled early challenges and chances, sparking a game alight. There was wonderful democracy about such tunnels: the sent-off player could be barracked up close; the hero's autograph could be easily obtained. This, and the relatable spontaneity of the run-out itself, served to thin the walls between player and supporter. There was never anywhere to hide.

28

LOAN MOVES BEING RARE

'ROVERS NET LOAN STAR' pronounced the local newspaper's back page. Then, in smaller letters 'Right-Back Arrives On One-Month Deal'. A footballer, parachuted in from a club far away. There was an air of exoticism. Such was the feeling in those times when permanent transfers were few, and loan deals a rare and intriguing phenomenon.

The borrowed footballer stirred feeling, created a frisson. He arrived often in a time of panic or crisis – 'we may look into the loan market', the vexed and wearied manager had admitted after another home defeat. Or he was summoned to answer the call of an injury emergency.

These subtexts, and the uncommon occurrence of a loan, gave him the air of a saviour. Here he was, changing kit in a telephone box and swooping in to play centre-half. Here he was, headhunted to play in goal after the regular keeper had sprained his wrist in training. Here he was, teeth sharpened to add some bite to a limp and overrun midfield. That his tenancy would not usually exceed four games, and often result only in a solitary appearance in the early rounds of the League Cup, mattered not: the thrill of the loan was in its announcement.

The loan player arrived with an aura of difference, some exchange student in a town twinning programme. Seldom, though, was there much of the continental or youthful about him. A loaned footballer was not a teenage prospect, sent away for a season to grow. He had no parent club, just owners who had grown tired of him. He was an old head, usually with a back catalogue of clubs. Farmed out by one manager who didn't want to keep him to another who needed him only for a short while, he lived now in purgatory. There was a library of such loanees, plucked from the shelves to type: stocky goalkeepers called Barry or Mark; bouncy-haired midfielders with three long-ago caps for England under-21s; gangly centre-forwards wearing tape around their ankles. On their debuts, they seemed to emit sparks when compared to existing squad members, foisting an energy upon the pitch as if alarmed by what they had found upon arrival. By the second half of their second game, they had naturalised and blended in with their foster team's inept manner.

Back in their proprietors' hold, short-term loanees rarely returned to first-team service, or were allowed to prove themselves. Many would soon be cadged out anew. Such loan moves were the beginning of a career's end, the first chimes of a retirement carriage clock.

29

CHOOSING WHO YOU'RE NEXT TO

Turnstile, Block, Row, Seat. Where you sit in the stand is a jeopardy, a fate decreed by computer. The numbers and letters contrived are random scratch card combinations, appropriately leading to annoyance and frustration. This is a tombola in which you may very well draw a deeply irritating person with whom you will have to sit for 90 minutes. Even selecting your own seat with a hopeful click of the mouse is a risk. There is no tiny seat icon marked: 'Warning: Gobshite'.

There are degrees of bad luck. All is relative. You may be able to move at half-time. It may be for one away game only. Or, dread slapped upon dread, this is your new season-ticket perch. A commitment fretted over and saved for, a summer's anticipation and giddy restlessness, all wrecked. You file along the row with August glee, locate your berth for the year. You sit and consider your view. A smile. So far so good, so far so good. Then he arrives at 3.05p.m. and howls through a lager mouth that the manager hasn't got a clue, and that nothing will ever change.

The thundering and eternal critic is just one type with whom you can be jammed, invisibly handcuffed by seating conventions. Irritants may also occupy surrounding seats, infiltrating your enjoyment of the game like spies whispering uncomfortable secrets. There are quiet cynics, muttering away throughout the game, a relentless campaign of 'They're not gonna score today' and 'I saw that coming'. There are experts, full of profound tactical insights and advice, not least 'Just bloody launch it.' There are quippers, executors of dire recurrent lines that made you want to burn your own ears off the first time they were inflicted upon you. There are personal space invaders with bulging knees and elbows like chimneys, leaving you sitting as if hunched in a suitcase. There are gawpers, looking hard in your direction should you dare break convention and sing along, Neighbourhood Watch committee men staring at new arrivals from behind the net curtains.

They were always there. In every old ground, over all seasons. That hotchpotch of humanity is, for all its exasperations, part of what makes a crowd. The difference was, you could once simply wander away. Drop a shoulder, jig to another part of the terrace. It was an open prison, free range not battery. There was always a place for you, in peace or song, alone or with your own kind of pilgrims.

30

MAIN-STAND CLOCKS

Hoisted lofty, an all-seeing eye. This animate moon helped shape tides of mood by dropping its small hand to three. It had a simple face. It was a functional decoration. Ostentation was left to the flags poked into the stand's roof. Pomp came from stately letters spelling out the club's name in a brass wreath around the clock. From the other side of the halfway line, its numbers were specks – hands told the story, drowsy conductors' batons.

Think of what it saw, imagine what it looked down upon. The hustle and bustle game of moustachioed Edwardians, roomy shorts dancing in the breeze. Men that were heroes in 1914 then mysteriously disappeared. Slick-haired swashbucklers making their names and throwing smiles onto thousands of faces. Nifty 60s schemers, pushing and caressing the ball through mud baths.

The main-stand clock saw more happenings, moved through more history, than God's own sundial. It ticked through times good and bad, it tocked through empty nights and summers when all other parts of the club snored. It chronicled the grass growing and watched white lines being painted, a never-ending refurbishment.

It was civic, a civilised presence, transposing onto the ground town-hall gravitas and memorial reverence. It marked and spanned every second, the silent second heartbeat of every fan present.

31

ONE-CLUB MEN

Did he dream of staying forever? Did he arrive as a wiry and acned teenager, signing his YTS forms and thinking: 'This place smells like home'? He may already have been a supporter, such scrawling on the dotted line an incredible, living dream, the keys to the sweet factory. Look back now at his signing-on photograph in an old matchday programme, and that feeling flickers from deep behind his eyes.

Or perhaps he was a little older, had worn other shirts that had never quite fitted. It was possible for the one-club man to have a hinterland that, in time, would be forgotten. Walking through the doors in his early 20s, did he feel that this was it, that something fitted, that he could belong here? Sometimes you just know.

His could be the story of thwarted ambition too, another romance of its own kind. That is, he ended up staying so long because the transfer he craved never came through, or was refused by his owners. There he was, the small-town boy who never got his big-city break, forever left to watch raindrops fall down the team-coach window and think about what might have been.

Whatever the backstory, the one-club man came to be cherished by supporters. His longevity, persistence and loyalty could mask the limitations of his game. If a centre-back, he was usually of the strapping type, always ready to use his forehead as a third foot. The ball was for clearing. Everything else was dilly-dally and show. If a centre-midfielder, he would be neat, unfussy and the scorer of one goal per season, always deflected and while the team were 2–0 down. A stalwart goalkeeper was on the shorter side and visibly panicked once the picking-up of back passes was outlawed, while a centre-forward threw his heavy body around when not dropped from the team and replaced by some fly-by-night signing. Most one-club men became, after a while, team captains, if only for hanging around long enough.

As the years fell away, these steadfast draught horses of the game saw their clubs change time and again. They outlived four or five managers, shook hands with and waved off half a century of new signings. Their strongest bonds were not with teammates but backroom staff and the fans who viewed them as the very fabric of the club. The one-club man was in the walls of the place. It became a social role, he a municipal footballer. He was a symbol of the area, the man for supermarket openings and the man to lead players in Christmas visits to the local children's ward. He was an ambassador in a captain's armband.

Then came the testimonial year. Awkward fundraising events. A game against foreign opposition, a bigger club or select 11. The award of a dubious penalty for him to score. Gate receipts from a thin post-season crowd. He may have played on the following season, and longer still, yet his career was now scraping towards its finale. Selected on fewer and fewer Saturdays, noted in his manager's interviews as being 'good to have around the place', these were the plunking tolls of a death knell. There may then have been a single season elsewhere, but he or football was never the same, the songs sung of an altogether different kind.

32

BEAMS AND IMPERFECT VIEWS

In the seats behind the beams, some supporters lengthened and fanned out their necks. A telescopic extra few centimetres enabled them to see a right-back curb tight wing play with a scything tackle. Some swayed forwards like bacon contorting in a frying pan just to watch the linesman's flag.

Those standing where a hoarding blocked sight of the touchline had the privilege of using their tiptoes. With an elbow landed softly on the shoulder of a neighbour, or two hands clamping a crush barrier, they gently ascended. It was almost pneumatic. Their toes helped them become a periscope, able to peer over the heads of others and witness penalty-area dragging and tugging as a corner was about to be taken.

These architectural eccentricities meant working for a sight of the unravelling match. Remaining still pushed areas of the pitch off the map. They were a mystery, a remote void to be imagined when the ball swung in their direction. It meant communal frustration, not least when catching hundreds of supporters by surprise as they took their places in an away enclosure. There was, too, a bleak enjoyment of this adversity; the same resigned incredulity which binds passengers in a static train carriage, darkly revelling in shared tuts and sarcasm.

Commonest among obstructions were wrought-iron beams. They seemed to have plunged from the sky, stalactite pillars as cold as icicles. Their roots were planted firmly in Victorian and Edwardian soil. They were simultaneously intricate and industrial, reflecting the graft and craftsmanship they presided over on the pitch. These girders sprouted through every wall and level of a club's sacred main stand, from tea room to boardroom. They supported a creaking structure, regal colonnades bolstering a bowing palace ceiling.

There were other hindrances. At the extremes of sideline stands, corrugated plastic walls grubbier than the Thames in winter. No amount of writhing or crinkling could bring vision of corner kicks, meaning the ball arrived in the box as a surprise, the cannonball of some unseen cubbyhole lower down the ship.

Sprinkled across the grounds of our land were intrusive outbuildings: tea huts, programme stalls and hatches into which £1 could be paid to upgrade from standing to a seated area. Such premises were as wildly varied as those coops, hutches and bunkers found on allotment fields – breeze-block huts, sheds in blazing club colours, brick and pallet-wood shacks. Stubbornly sticking with a terrace corner perch upon which these buildings infringed meant peeping around their corners or over their roofs. It gave the homely feel of peering across a relative to catch sight of the television.

33

SPONSORED PLAYERS' CARS

The players' car park. Long a grey garden of intrigue, a stable for supporter nosiness. The place where autographs were collected. The venue of brief encounters with heroes, treasured exchanges still recalled 30 years later. No other car park can compete; it is like comparing a rich ocean to a puddle.

So infrequent were interactions with footballers that the tarmac became symbolic. The loss of open car parks to under-stadium tunnels and barrier security means the curbing of such wondrous meetings. Stolen seconds of equality, when footballers appear to us as actual humans, are disappearing.

While stadium architecture and fluorescent jackets restrict us, no longer can we make awkward eye contact with players' relatives. Gone is the thrill of peeking through the manager's car window to see a packet of wine gums by the gear stick. Lost is the post-match drift out of the stadium of retired players, and of a wild but good-natured few heckling the suited referee.

Where now players board their blacked-out wagons, this was once the place to sight a player flat-packing himself into his small sponsored car. In their vehicles bloated with labels and livery, it was impossible not to. 'David Kerslake Drives a Fiat Uno' or 'Des Walker Only Drives Rovers' blasted white-lettered stickers on both front doors.

There would be more proclamations of the proud sponsor, usually a local car dealership, splattered across every surface, an italicised phone number too. These vehicles were never Jaguar or Mercedes, and always Capri or Cosworth. Cars supporters could relate to, driven by players they had spoken with.

Sponsored cars rendered players unmissable. Catching sight of one away from the ground – or, deepest joy, pulling level in a traffic jam – was even greater than those cherished car-park moments. Long reigned local stories of children chasing players' cars down suburban streets, a Pied Piper trail with exhaust fumes replacing musical notes.

34

HOMES WITH VIEWS INTO THE GROUND

In the corner of the ground was a gap. This empty space between one stand and another meant real life was visible, though confined by a brick wall or steel gates. Sometimes the barricade withheld a straggly collection of trees, sometimes an unseen road running by, tapping out flat background rhythms. Loftier grounds that clawed onto hill edges allowed blurry visions of spires, chimneys and rooftops. Elsewhere, faraway hills lined the stomach of a valley. Fixing upon them during a particularly galling home defeat both remedied the soul with perspective and intensified one's feeling of helplessness.

There was no greater corner distraction than a place of residence. Whether redbrick terrace, tower block of flats or semi-detached villa, a home from which the inside of a football ground could be seen was effortlessly appealing. Here were living rooms facing the corner flag, kitchens from which eye contact could be made with a floodlight, bedroom windows that looked out upon your favourite view through every sun and moon. Christ, you wouldn't have needed a television had you lived there. The landing balcony of a high rise was a gallery terrace, an airship's view of heaven.

It was difficult to comprehend quite how utopian life within those walls must have been: how much of the pitch could they see – a snippet, a quarter, the goalmouth? What did a goal sound like if you were in the bath? Had the ball smashed a window, shocked carp in the pond or dented the fuchsias? What did the pitch look like on a weekday morning, or at 3.30a.m.? Could a defeat be forgotten by drawing the curtains? From their homes could those residents see the life of a ground, its moods and seasons. They had 365-day season tickets. They had the privilege of the daytime sightseer and the thrilling access of the night-watchman. When dark fell, they were art-gallery attendants left alone to marvel at treasures framed by turnstiles and grandstands. And yet you suspected that none of them were really that bothered.

Such gaps have been lost to hermetically sealed stadiums that close our eyes for us. It is hard now to spot, too, holes in the fence or cracks in the gate. Formerly, between the decaying paint of two sturdy oak panel doors could be seen a slither of the ground's insides. Standing back, it gave you a glimpse of a ground's layers and shades: cinder track, green turf, red seats, stand roof, sky. In this crevice was the colour chart of football. If you were glancing in on matchday, added to this were the flickering figures that quickly appeared then disappeared; footballers as the contents of some technicolour zoetrope.

Those of us who felt like this about such stealthy views, who were in these circumstances always children at the toyshop window, were guilty of a kind of mania. We were desperate to see inside from an unfamiliar angle. We shared that much with those who clambered up on stand roofs or hauled themselves into trees to watch sold-out games. Such desperation placed a higher value upon a ground, enriched it. It stated that spectacle lay within, that a promised land was touchable. When you glimpsed inside a football ground from somewhere unusual, or merely imagined doing such a thing, it made Narnia even more enchanting.

35

TURNSTILE OPERATORS

As kick-off ticked near, there were queuing minutes to contemplate what appeared ahead. Shuffling towards the turnstile helped you swallow the spectacle. Surroundings became firmer, immersive. Above the entrance, gate prices – Adult, OAP, Child. Rarely did admission fees bloat beyond a tenner. Over the years, a £7 had given way to an £8 and then an £8.50, each waning figure visible beneath the next. Old numbers were ghosts of seasons gone by, retreating whispers.

The entrance itself, when you contemplated it, was a fine margin rather than a doorway. Slender to the point of disappearing, it was a portal through which supporters pinched and filed. Inside this stubby ginnel they came to a halt, their hips engaged with a cast-iron buffer. This was only the public part of a turnstile, a rectangular bulbous loop. It was adjoined to an ornate structure of bars and levers, beauty disguised by the dark like some remarkable deep-sea fish. Most turnstiles proudly declared their parentage and finest traits: Deluce's Patent Rush Preventive Turnstile – Sole Makers WT Ellison & Co Limited, Irlams o' th' Height, Manchester.

The supporter saw only a crescent table of sheet metal or oak and the mesh that ran up from it. This shrouded the turnstile operator as if he or she were a priest about to take Confession. At its centre was a small horseshoe-arch opening, a mouse hole for pushing through gate money. On the dark side were crooked piles of coins ready to be issued with an accompanying grunt for those fans paying with a note. Rough hands or daintier shivering ones cocooned in fingerless gloves prodded forward change and slid across a small square ticket.

A supporter's eyes stayed mainly on these hands, only occasionally straying upwards. A roving glance would encounter turnstile operators never wavering from their task, never lifting their neck straight. Many were older men with wiry hair who seemed unreasonably tall and bulky, caged bears in donkey jackets. None spoke, though not all were grumpy – these, after all, were often the people complicit in allowing a child to get a 'lift over' for free. There was also in every ground a troop of cheerful women in their 60s, each of them ready to turn severe on a late teen attempting to pass for a concession.

This turnstile loyal saw it all: the proud dad taking his daughter to her first game; the early arrivals with flasks of Oxo; the rowdy singers hardly breaking lyrical stride as they passed through; the latecomers, faces crimson and chests pulsating from a dash to the ground.

The operator stepped on a pedal, the supporter heaved and the turnstile whirled them into pleasant bedlam. Such fleeting exchanges and ritual encounters made matchday a social tapestry. The rat-a-tat-tats and clacks of turnstiles were melodious; the buzz of an automatic barcode entrance is like replacing birdsong with a fire alarm.

36

SHABBY TRAINING GROUNDS

They were seldom seen, caught in photographs or occasional television clips only. Even then, training grounds were incidental, the fuzzy home-made backdrops of village pantomimes. It added to their allure as unreachable and forbidden territories.

In these images, focus dropped upon a foreground footballer jumping over a metal frame, socks rolled down and crumpled training top immobile, or mid-volley, thrusting the ball to an unseen teammate. A tracksuit-clad manager was sometimes captured here too, jabbing and pointing like a drunk arguing in a mirror. No matter the reality, when recalled in the mind he had always a whistle around his neck.

Staring into those backgrounds, it was possible to decipher the features and lines of this unknown world. All training grounds appeared to be squatted among suburban estates. Their unkempt grass was surrounded first by a fence occasionally garnished with barbed wire, and then two-storey semi-detached homes. In a distant corner loomed the lonely frames of spartan changing rooms, desolate igloos.

Detectable were the trimmings of civilian life – lampposts and telegraph poles beyond tinny goalposts. A keen eye could spot shrubbery, a keen mind could imagine the many stray footballs that had rolled into bushes and been forced into abrupt retirement. It must have been like an abandoned battlefield within, balls of various ages laid limp, some flat, some wilting.

There was captivation as well for those of us supporting teams with no fixed training abode. Decoding images inspired different questions: which salty beach, school-field quagmire or barren prison ground were they stomping up and down this time?

Though many training ground names were known – The Cliff, Lower Gigg, Harlington,

Bellefield, Platt Lane – they remained mysterious places. A chosen few young fans had visited, their autograph books paraded as evidence, and yet these venues still seemed unreachable. Football was more hidden. Knowing less meant pure, tantalising curiosity and the magic of filling in gaps with your imagination.

37

CHARACTERFUL CAPTAINS' ARMBANDS

There was no orthodoxy, no standard issue and no logo or sponsor, just whatever worked best on that day for that particular captain. It sometimes appeared that armbands were fashioned from the handiest suitable item. Medical dressings could be used, grubby bandages coiled around a bicep in the manner of a St John Ambulance volunteer's first effort. Some skippers unsnarled a ribbon of duct tape, numbing their humerus in a crude brassard. Elasticated fabrics were curved into a cylinder shape and fettered together, and cotton sweatbands reversed and heaved upwards from the wrist.

For some, such improvisation would never do. They were content only with a conventional band of elastic marked 'Captain' or simply 'C'. Such items were visible in many town-centre sports shops, displayed in glass cabinets as if museum treasures. Stitched into cloth, there was gravitas in that word 'captain'. Those letters gave rank and station, and marked their wearer as responsible, a commander. They gave him the authority and appearance of a traffic constable, dignified and in control, at least until a two-footed lunge of retribution was required.

How an armband was worn told you something of its holder. A ligature high up the limb spoke of a barking figurehead, probably a centre-half, with military tendencies and a dark secretive love of butterfly stitches. His fierce approach to the coin toss contrasted with the more casual wearer. This bohemian creative type allowed his armlet to droop around the elbow. At any moment it threatened to drop to the ground like a postman's rubber band. It suggested he was relaxed about being captain, thought nothing of the symbolism involved. His life would not change because of an elasticated offcut. There he sauntered around in the centre-circle, an air-raid warden never believing that bombs would fall.

38

PROVINCIAL BUSINESSMAN OWNERS

Looking at photographs, you felt that you could guess what he smelled like. Tobacco would be there, accompanied by the lingering scent of Scotch or cognac, poured at half-time from a crystal decanter. Sweet aftershave would be hovering too, and subtly medicinal notes of Brylcreem. His hair – and boy was he proud of its virile thickness – would be cladded with the stuff, all part of his cultivated rigid demeanour.

Beneath a scratchy static suit in beige, brown or grey were possibly braces, tie clips and sleeve garters, and certainly a sizable belly nurtured by a thousand Sunday roasts and fundraising dinners. No-nonsense, substantial, common sense ... all of these were essential terms for the provincial businessmen owner. Nowt fancy, nowt flash, a life and a club run within its means. A man who, according to himself, said it like it was.

Each was blessed with a solid first name: Sam, John, Bob, Tony, Terry, Bill, Ken or Reg. Some achieved the sacred reward of official recognition – Sir Anthony or Sir Richard. Their businesses had started locally and frequently spread throughout the county. Waste disposal, kitchen wholesale, paper mills, engineering, catering, haulage, construction, brewing … in their locales they were big players. Some, it was rumoured, were multi-millionaires.

Whether from local pride, 'putting something back' or through a quaint breed of megalomania, they had branched out into other areas. Their names appeared on the board lists of trusts, charities and associations. They were involved in guilds, chambers and even at the Freemasons' Hall. They dabbled in municipal politics, golfed with the mayor. Buying the football club was an extension, the pinnacle even, of this. It was the civic thing to do. Here would be an asset that, outwardly, this owner was building and maintaining for local citizens – a football club was the 20th century's version of an eccentric branch line at the height of Victorian railway mania.

Ownership did not make for universal popularity among supporters. Adulation was rare, grudging respect the default position. Fans craved flamboyant transfers. There was no glee in steady shoestring governance. The owner stubbornly continued above a perpetual clamour for undefined change and progress. It was an area in which he could not win, as with his approach to the hiring and firing of managers; sack early and he was rash, show patience and he was overly loyal.

So it was that he continued on his upright course. Greying years of Saturdays passed with him upon his padded throne overlooking the halfway line. It seemed as if he would die in situ, the tired king. Money, new money, said otherwise. Cheque zeros enough to please club, family and owner spelled the end. Out from the designated space reversed his racing-green Jaguar XJ-S. In rolled the modern age.

39

CARETAKER MANAGERS

Here was a gentler being than the modern interim manager. He sniffs a shot at the full-time role should three or four wins from five be clawed. The traditional caretaker manager had no such vaulting ambition. His only aspiration was to blanch once more into the background. He would be called upon again, after the next managerial lynching. The caretaker manager was a supply teacher in an initialled jumper.

He was a club man, as immovable as the claggy boardroom carpet. He had usually played for the team, and had even watched them as a boy. Then, after retirement came various dilettante backdrop positions – kit man, novice physiotherapist, youth coach, and finally everlasting, loyal manager's number two. Through each position and through his caretaker stints, there was sartorial consistency: always shorts and socks, always that jumper or training top. Had he worn a suit, supporters would have presumed court or a death in the family.

The protocol must have become familiar. A landline bellowing in the evening, 'Who on earth's that calling at this hour?' The chairman's voice. The boss is no more. The caretaker is needed. Can he steady the ship for a while? Of course he can, right until the new man is ready.

In his first team selection, there would be no overhaul but certainly a dabbling and telling change or two – the frozen-out winger brought in to thaw, the old-head midfielder back as a solidifying element. For the supporter, watching him take the lead in the dugout could be discombobulating, as if statues had awoken and were suddenly on the march. A narrow, battling defeat and the chiselling of a 0–0 draw would follow. Such outcomes would be proof enough for the caretaker that the rot had been stopped. He would assert that much in ever-awkward media interviews.

Life still was about that next manager. Our man would step down for him and become immediately loyal. He would have no say nor choice in the appointment: it was an arranged marriage. That does not mean his was a forlorn, undervalued vocation – he was trusted implicitly by owner and board, the figure players could talk to, a linkman diplomat needed to ease the new gaffer in.

With fanfare that gaffer arrived. The caretaker eased silently back to his old life, working away in the background like a dad washing the Christmas dishes.

40

PAPER TICKETS

I have, in a drawer, a large envelope wadded with old match tickets. Saved from the late 1980s to mid-1990s, these paper chits are quite glorious in their endless variety. There is very little uniform about them, save for stock details of fixture, entrance cost and stand. They are as different to each other as one fingerprint is to the next.

Derby County is a centimetre's length from being a perfect square. There are three print colours: background flourishes in sticky-plaster cream-brown, text in gloaming blue and blurred black. For Notts County Football Club, silver letters embossed at the head of a shepherd's-delight red. Two magpies are rendered shiny, a danger to themselves. Particulars are recounted in pixels so archetypal that it feels like the faint hums and wheezes of an old printer can be heard. Going further, on one edge Grimsby Town have left in place a perforated strip of dot-matrix holes. Phone 0898 121576 to 'Listen To The Manager After The Match', it says beside them.

At Manchester City they wish for you to 'Take Up Your Position At Least 45 Minutes Prior To Kick-Off', at Bolton Wanderers 30 and at Hibernian 15. Newcastle United repeat themselves a hundred times over, that hallowed name filling the background in a rolling wave pattern, a North Sea and River Tyne shanty. York – a landscape strip the size of a toddler's foot – has at its centre one of the gates to the city, gracious historical pedigree. Hull City throw speech marks around "Barclays League" and give directions to West Stand Staircase W in a typeface previously used to declare war.

Those same Tigers offer a delicious promise: Plan of Ground Overleaf. I turn each ticket around and it is the same. In keeping with their front covers, every design is unique. All possess wistful charm that makes me sigh enough to change the wind. Here is Selhurst Park, its Holmesdale and Arthur Wait Stands in angular 3D, seating blocks marked by capital letters. St James' Park is sketched as if the fruit of a dream scribbled onto a pad next to the bed. Highbury is an art-deco plaything. Others take more functional overhead views. Everything fans out from the pitch, which at Elland Road has no halfway line or centre circle, the Baseball Ground no markings at all, and Boothferry Park the four barren points of a compass where white lines should be.

Touching these slices of paper throws me up in the air and lands me in another world. Ruffling through the textures of my enveloped pile gives the misty thrill of kicking rustling leaves. I will never feel the same about generic card slips or print-at-home tickets.

41

PLAYER BRAWLS

Football supporters revel in the forbidden and the unfortunate. The referee falling over is a moment of high fiesta. A ball scaling the stand roof never to be seen again courts not sympathy but a cheer. The occurrences we are not supposed to enjoy are wholeheartedly celebrated. If a commentator deplores appalling scenes not suitable for family viewing, the supporter knows exactly where to look. No fan has ever protected his eyes from a pitch invader. What the camera turns away from, the spectator looks towards.

Now lost to petty squabbles and handbags that end in handshakes, the multi-player brawl was the finest example of this. In the ground or on television, it was impossible not to stare and bay for more. It was not that we wanted cold and terrifying violence. Joy rested both in the slapstick ruckus on offer, and the knowledge that football's prim authority figures would be gurgling with outrage. Nothing could top looking from a distance upon someone else's trouble. We summoned the spirit of playground war cries and stood around, watching: *fight fight fight fight*.

A brawl did not come from nowhere. The game had been niggly, pocked with needle and edge. The turf rumbled. Rain helped, oiling the surface to allow greater traction. Each slide tackle was later and stormier than the previous.

Then, the moment of combustion. Throbbing his foot through the ball, a full-back propels it clear. A second after it deserts his laces, two feet carve in and greet his ankles. A winger's revenge for an earlier mangle; the choppy haggling of a defender and an attacker. Full-back writhes, winger raises arms of innocence. In they steam, drunks towards the dancefloor. First to arrive is the brigand midfielder teammate of the fallen. Suddenly ordained with blistering pace, his hands are around the neck of the perpetrator before the referee has tooted his desperate first peep. Seven or eight more scrappers have now piled in, their differently shirted arms pushing at one another like berserk oil pumpjacks. The referee's whistle continues to hiss. Neither he nor the linesmen now on the pitch can change anything. More players arrive. Side battles spark up, all jostles and grabs, whiplash and thick ears. Through the storm, the crowd rallies and is engrossed. Meanwhile, beneath the legs of this quarrelling centipede, the fouled full-back remains grounded.

At last peacemakers arrive. Captains remember their duty and managers with their coaches stride onto the pitch. They pull players apart, occasionally joining in by accident. Things slow, arms are dislodged and used for pointing instead. Players sling accusations and show the officials their cuts and rashes. A lone guerrilla tries to fight on and is restrained by his goalkeeper. The referee calls in his favoured culprits and flashes yellow cards with the flourish of a composer conducting his own beloved sonata.

Television highlights and Sunday newspaper reports will claim that this brawl disgraced and overshadowed the match. The supporter will think otherwise.

42

PIXELATED SCOREBOARDS

It is a futile exercise, but a happy indulgence. On a November afternoon as rain collapses down I find myself staring out of the window thinking about it. Or, trying to get to sleep at night, I mentally sketch details in the vain hope that it will enter my slumber as a dream. Here is the confession: I am constructing in my head the perfect football ground.

Rarely does it have many modern trappings. It is more the type of stadium seen through the eyes and pencils of Janet Ahlberg, or one painted by L.S. Lowry. It has a grand main stand with delicate brickwork on the outside and wrought-iron gates in a corner. Tucked into that stand are a modest club shop and several window hatches which constitute the ticket office, each with a small arched gap cut out of the glass for transactions. There is a cheerful wooden sign denoting an entrance for 'Players and Officials'. A walk through the gates takes us to a behind-goal stand, named the something-Road End. Less ornate than the main stand, its pebbledash walls and pencil-thin turnstiles with gate prices written above still have charm. There is a similar enclosure opposite, though this time with a roof, and a grandstand runs the length between them in corrugated steel and fibreglass as far as the misty eye can see.

Within the walls of my utopia, those two ends are terraced, with radiant crush barriers evenly scattered across their concrete steps as if visual echoes of the goals on the pitch. The roofed stand has a refreshments kiosk beyond the back row, the unroofed a brick hut near a corner flag. On darker afternoons, the light within both glows warm, giving the joy of spotting a Christmas tree in someone's front room from the street. They serve tea, which splashes from urns and scolds lips, and beige snacks with serviettes folded around them. The grandstand has seats in its upper tier, and a terrace beneath, the very height of civilisation. The main stand is tightly packed with seats of varnished wood. At the back is a glass box from where announcements are made, and the scoreboard is programmed.

There is always a scoreboard, in this imaginary case clipped to the roof behind the goal. It is always of the vintage variety in technology that for so long bridged footballs old and new, the son looking up to the same board his dad once did. Whether using filament lightbulbs or pixel dots and specks, such scoreboards shimmered, adding a restrained sort of showbiz fizzle to pallid grounds. There was a touch of class and authority in their chalkboard-black backgrounds, and a glamour in their beaming and sparky orange or yellow lettering.

Each bulb or pixel played its part in the dance. A basic formation meant the displaying of the two teams' names, with nicknames, abbreviations and even 'Visitors' used just to remind everyone whose theatre this was. Often, dots marked the space between the end of a team's name and the amount of goals they had or hadn't scored, a gentle, patient way to reiterate bad news. Late arrival at a game made the scoreline function useful, but a board's most frequently important declaration was that of how many minutes had elapsed. As the game slipped onwards, those digits were watched in anxious scrutiny through all but the most emphatic of results. At 1–0 down the seconds rolled as if being channelled through an infant's hasty counting; 2–1 up and they seemed to move backwards.

There could be details and flourishes beyond these. Most dramatically, a blazing, flashing scoreboard decrying 'GOAL!' amidst shooting-star graphics became part of the wondrous carnival of scoring, alongside unhinged celebrations and the goal-getter's name being read aloud. That said, there were few lonelier places to be than some far-flung away end watching this light-and-sound show erupt after your team had conceded. Onwards rumbled the pixel scoreboard show, through half-time birthday wishes for 'Vicky, 8 today, Love Mum, Dad and Our Paul' stuttering across the screen, stick men kicking a ball, robotic 'Mr Chips' figures waving scarves, a 'Come on, City!' accompanying a corner, and pairs of hands clapping the team onto the pitch.

Ah, to see the lights once more.

43

HUTS ON STAND ROOFS

What were they like inside? Did these curious lairs contain furniture, fittings? They were to us supporters another unseen part of the ground, more imagined spaces to go alongside boardrooms, managers' offices and players' lounges. We populated them with magic and wonder. In our daydreams, they never reeked of damp. Those huts and bunkers clamped to stand roofs were unknown, impossible theatres – Punch and Judy booths whose curtains would never open. Those perched inside may as well have been sitting in the clouds.

We guessed who they were, the chosen hermits. Local-radio commentators in their cherished spots; visiting national counterparts rolling their eyes at the facilities. Public-address announcers squinting to see who was making way for a last-ditch substitute. A lone cameraman swishing his lens from one end to the other through an afternoon of humped clearances and hit-and-hopes. Each imagined soul had scaled rusty iron ladders, put blind faith in doddery gangway rails and crouched through the gantry door. We knew it was hardly pleasant, and yet would gladly have climbed a school gymnasium rope to join them.

No two eyries were the same. At Oakwell, a lipstick-red birdwatching shed directly above the tunnel. At Saltergate, an ashen pillbox. At Burnden Park, a cerulean bolt hole not unlike a shipping container with window panels. At Prenton Park, a bus stop with aerials. At Filbert Street, a cabin protruding from the roof like a bird poking its head out of an eggshell. At Ayresome Park, a bounty: two separate cubicles with space for a camera in-between.

Each hut languished high above the stand opposite. Soaring over the ground must have given a godly thrill. In wilder moments, it could have been possible to feel like some grand narrator overseeing a story unfurl. Here was a vantage ripe for mass observation and rounded insight. Being so removed, however, may have invited more troubling, existential thoughts. From this elevated position could be seen the outside world, ready to intrude at any point. To stare into the distance would have been to dice with reality.

No part of a ground seemed to go unused. Bivouac tea stations and first-aid hovels were assembled if a few empty yards were spotted. Extra seating areas were fixed to the sides of stands like scaffold limpets. Stand roofs hosted not only huts, but vast and ornate advertisements for local industries. This was an age of character and difference.

44

REGIONAL HIGHLIGHTS PROGRAMMES

Gary Hamilton. Tony Mowbray. Bernie Slaven. I am turning the pages of an old autograph book. Stuart Ripley. Stephen Pears. Colin Cooper. These scrawls remain familiar. I collected them many times over, copied them onto my school books. Even so, in helter-skelter lettering, young me has labelled each signature at the foot of the page.

The same goes for figures my dad pushed me towards outside various grounds after a match. Then, they were impossibly old men, distractions from obtaining Gary Parkinson's autograph for the 14th time. Now though, thanks to that cluttered categorising, I can see that I possess the autographs of Wilf Mannion and George Hardwick, Peter Lorimer and Billy Bremner. Such gems must be mined for – there are also reams of late 20th century lower-division midfielders. And, I note as I turn, one 'Duncan Wood'.

It takes a few seconds for me to remember that Duncan Wood was a sports presenter on Tyne Tees Television. Within a few further seconds, I can recall his avuncular Wearside metre. He was able to convey news of another Middlesbrough defeat with the kind of compassion and pity I needed. He was, in our north-eastern world, someone whose autograph was worth the paper it was written on. Wood's sympathetic tidings reached us through sports bulletins during the evening news, and, crucially, in sporadic Sunday and midweek football-highlights shows.

Here was a land in which most regions had their own Wood and their own version of such a programme. Footballing audiences knew little of what existed elsewhere. A face well known on one side of the Pennines – and ridiculed in chant, even – was a stranger on the other. When a slot was bestowed upon them, Tyne Tees, Granada, Yorkshire, Anglia, Meridian, Carlton and the rest bombarded us with local goals. Their programme titles alone electrified dull Sunday-lunchtime and midweek-bedtime television listings: *The London Match, Granada Soccer Night, Goals on Sunday, Midweek Sports Special, Match of the Week, Your Game, Football Special, Soccer Sunday, Shoot...* Inside this Mecca, there would be extended highlights of one or two games, and then an unleashing of action, inaction and incident from your very own pocket of the country. Beyond normal rivalries, it was enough to sow lifelong soft spots and loyalty to the other stars of your show, especially if they were in a lower division.

Each channel with its own show, each show with its own graphics, theme tune, presenters and commentators. Each region with its band of featured clubs. What bounteous, complex terrain.

45

LUXURY, SUPERFLUOUS PLAYERS

He was one of those kids that everyone had heard of. One week he had scored eleven in a match, the next nine. He had chipped the keeper from the halfway line, someone at school said, and got one with his shoulder. Playing against him was an exercise in pointlessness. Thinking yourself close and ready to tackle, you would look up to see him suddenly 10 yards away. He was an optical illusion. With his instep alone, he could welter the ball harder than your chubbiest teammate, whose own shots had stung raw many a thigh. It was like he was made of something different to the rest of you.

He wasn't long for your level of football. Pretty soon he would disappear, captured by a professional club. From then onwards, he was playing a different sport. All the rest of you could do was trace his career, first through occasional mentions in the local paper, and then in grounds across the land. Teenage jealousy bowed away to adult pride – 'I played against him once', we said from the stands.

Competitive football kept his extravagance in check. It was an education, watching him go from centrepiece to drifter. Everything had once revolved around him. Now he could be seen prowling in the centre-circle, desperate to fling his magic upon a game happening around him. His indolence was accommodated because what he could do was worth waiting for.

There was opulence in his first touch. To watch him bring down a ball was to gargle champagne. He accepted a wildly over-hit pass as if it were a ping-pong ball landing upon a beanbag. This control made the noise of an expensive car door closing. He did not just beat defenders, he abolished them. There was splendour in the way he did so. His shoulder drops and deft turns were rare and golden trappings. No shot of his was opportune or scuffed, no goal fortunate. Only extravagant attempts were pursued, outlandish curlers with no respect for trigonometry,

35-yard beezers that seemed to leave a fork of lightning in their wake.

He had no exact position, no duty other than creation. His game was not rounded; his tackling was grim. He had no function beyond entertainment, joy and distraction: football's highest calling.

46

BALD PLAYERS

There was something heartening about footballers who looked like maths teachers. They were easy to relate to. Here was a familiar breed. Some even reminded you of your dad. Their welcoming faces were crisscrossed with moustaches and creases. Most of them were probably only in their 20s, and yet appeared as if they had fought in the war. There was very little difference between the men you saw through the humdrum week and those you rested your hopes upon when Saturday came. The main divergence was that they wore shorts to work, and even then many looked awkward, as if dreaming of a sensible pair of Burton trousers.

Nobody typified this normality more than the bald player. Had he turned up in your street, selling fish or come to collect an insurance payment from your parents, you would not have recognised him. He was ordinary, routine, workaday. This enhanced supporter admiration – there was a sense that he was one of us, playing for us. There are uplifting moments in life when a friend or colleague astonishes you with a hidden talent. Here was a man of the same world as you that could do so every week. This was reinforced by the fact that, rather than cropping to voguish stubble, the bald footballer often left hair remnants in place. There would be a u-bend panel of ginger wool, or a crest of mousy fur. Or a wispy strand like the string on a lost helium balloon.

Oddly, bald players were rarely centre-forwards, as if that were too flamboyant a position for this modest way of being. They were, by and large, thinning goalkeepers, barren full-backs and desolate centre-midfielders. Their play was marked by the calm, studied and methodical efficiency of a locksmith. The ball launched from their pates with ballistic intensity, and made the noise of lightning dissecting a telegraph pole. It was a rhapsody of the mundane. How little music there is in a hair transplant.

47

GOAL NETS WITH PERSONALITY

The luscious hoops of St James' Park, the strident rafters of Wembley or The Dell's shallow bookends: it was once possible to identify a ground by its goal nets. Nothing was standardised or flat-pack, all iron and string furniture was distinct. At the end of every pitch, a club's own interpretation of what a goal frame and net should be. A small detail that showered yet more personality, charm and difference upon our places of worship.

For some, a loop welded to any point in the upper quarter of a goalpost. The shape of each team's specimen varied: a stretched capital D; the handle of a giant gravy boat; the curve in a shepherd's crook; an industrial clothes hanger; a monkey's ears. For others, the prongs of a stanchion at each side of the goal, flying buttresses in acrylic cladding. The purpose of each approach was to shoo the net outwards and away from the goal line.

As a happy consequence of individualism, no two goals appeared to have the same dimensions. At some grounds, the net sagged and its drape could tickle a goalkeeper's neck. Elsewhere, he could fall back in despair and still not scrape his head against the net's perimeter. Those more cavernous goal nets made perfect impromptu boxing rings for brawls between defenders holding on to the ball, and opponents seeking to abscond with it back to the halfway line.

It was a similarly disparate tale with the netting itself. Each goal net was a unique twine tapestry. There were coarse hexagons the width of coffee mugs, crooked squares apparently borrowed from fishing vessels, and tiny intricate sequences like spider's webs. These were the delicate lace patterns of our Saturdays, our beloved wedding veils. Always were nets chalky white, though glimpses of exotically striped continental versions raced the pulse.

With some models, there could be a perfect collision, a splendid chemical reaction between net and frame when impacted by the ball. This contrived to enhance a goal scored and make recollections of it sharper. A finely balanced equation of sag and tautness would result in a shot bulging and rippling the net with artistic grace, impacting like a cannonball in a parachute and then spinning downwards like a spent firework. A rigidly tense net would offer instant rebound, and the chance for scorer or teammate, or anguished goalkeeper, to hammer the ball back into the mesh or off the pitch. A net with material to spare would result in bunched-up plumage on the ground, so that the ball floated inwards and stayed put, a butterfly in stickyweed. It would fall to the keeper, humiliated enough, to set it free, craned over to resemble a fishwife mending a lobster creel.

To stand behind your team's goal in its unique form was to come home.

48

THE MANY SCENTS OF MATCHDAY

We hover over cobbles, seeking a parking space. Up and down grids of terraced streets my dad drives, the car a cross-stitch needle. A few early Middlesbrough supporters walk towards Ayresome Park. When we pass them while driving in the opposite direction, it douses me in panic, makes me feel like the boy whose parents have forgotten Christmas. Finally, an opening is found. Dad reverses into the space and turns off the engine. When it falls stone dead, so too does Radio Five, suspended until teatime.

It already smells like a matchday outside of the car. The air gives a knowing wink, speckled as it is with food-wagon aromas. The scents specific to our matchday afternoons unravel. They are almost visible, like tempting vapours in a cartoon. On Essex Street, batter and condiments ooze from the chippy, tickling nostrils. There are wafts of herbs and spices in the newsagent with an adjoining domestic kitchen. My salt-and-vinegar crisps are different here, more pungent and stinging. Fanzine print and paper smell like some tropical and perishing vegetable. I push my nose into my paper bag filled with a quarter of Midget Gems and they smell of Saturday.

Inside the ground, there are further odours. Bovril smells like a museum exhibit about World War Two. In the toilets, urinal-block soaps are overcome by their target. There is little reason to linger in the shadowy grotto beneath the stand, and further matchday fragrances await us upstairs.

It is the tobacco that I remember most. Tart cigarette smoke dawdling in the air, a lethargic ghost. Roll-ups like burnt liquorice. The earthy cigars of the man we sat next to, and sour old men with pipes. Tobacco lined the atmosphere. Fingers struck matches and thumbs rolled lighter wheels from kick-off until injury time. Our Hamlet neighbour, I noticed, always lit up after a goal, post-coital. On Teesside – and other towns and cities had their own version, indeed other grounds their own smells – there was a nasal accompaniment of industrial perfume. The tar and burnt car-tyre scents of graft and chimneys complemented and underpinned the tobacco.

Each of these fragrances defined our matchdays. Football smelled more then. It was identifiable by its scents. Time has made them float away. In this case, Middlesbrough moved grounds, the chippy and newsagent closed, Midget Gems were sealed in plastic packets, smoking was banned, and industry largely crushed. The theme, though, is universal.

It should not be possible to feel sentimental about some of these smells. Yet when I pass a shivering officer worker dragging on a certain species of cigarette, or enter an old room that reeks of Hamlets, I ache with nostalgia. Inhaling these evocative scents fires up yearning. All that remains is the saintly catering van, a pale reminder of when so much more of football could be breathed in.

49

UNDERSTATED GOAL CELEBRATIONS

Not many of us crave the high sensation and spectacle which now surrounds football. Moments, goals and players are garlanded with undue brouhaha, all swooshing sound effects, overdone headlines and flimsy superlatives. Everything is the greatest or the gravest. Player injuries are discussed on radio news programmes. Statistical data cloys conversation and screens where once it was non-existent beyond league tables and top goalscorers' charts. No one in our old world was guilty of seeing things that were not there, adding system modelling and mathematical posturing to a game of chaos, wonder and blessed incompetence. Put simply, football felt more like it belonged to us.

This stiller world was embodied in players' understated goal celebrations. Here were climactic moments responded to without choreography, ego or hands lifted to ears in front of the away end. A scoring player could seem modest to the point of embarrassment. It was as if he did not want to take all of the glory and wished to silently convey that a goal belonged to everyone. There was poignancy in this reaction for those on the other side of the advertising hoardings. A scorer's lack of self-congratulation tacitly acknowledged that a goal was a supporter's moment. Here was the star actor, pointing to the audience during curtain-call applause.

His celebration was rarely more flamboyant than the raising of an arm. Perhaps he was taking time to drink in the roar of the crowd, even to look at those smiling faces. He would take the back pats and rigid hugs of teammates, the feeble handshakes and the cupped taps to the back of his head. Then, a jog back to the halfway line, where he could catch breath with hands rested above knees. He looked to the ball now moored on the centre-spot and gave inward thanks for what it had given him, and what it had given that crowd.

In truth, he deserved to be more exultant. None of us would have minded. Instead, he was left to revel in a goal in his own time, staring into space among the racket of the communal bath. There could now rise across his face the grin of a fulfilled man.

50

HEROES

Up there on your bedroom wall, in posters with tatty corners. A hero to you, a god in your town. Captured in motion ascending for a header or ball tethered to his foot by invisible magic, it was hard to see what set him apart. But you knew. You felt it. He was the one who made everything alright, the one who sculpted dreams. He was the one who tied the tongue of autograph-hunters, the one whose name thousands sung like a hymn and a war cry. On this paragon were hopes rested and wishes cast.

Did you age and lose awe, or did his type disappear? There are now global heroes and names on shirt backs. This backyard idol, though, has vanished. Players don't loiter long enough to become familiar, endearing and then venerated. Each club is a fling and not a true love. A modern supporter will never know this supreme affection. Bewitched by its spell, it can feel as if the adored player has a halo above his head when he takes possession of the ball. A player now can turn heads and sprinkle joy, but transfers soon make a faint memory of him, the scent of Regal Kings on a book that once belonged to your granddad.

Heroes earned their status for different reasons. Some were a certain breed – the stalwart, the jinking genius, the hard man. Others became so for stand-alone accomplishments that prettified steady careers; cup-final or derby goals. Many teams were endowed by cult heroes, worshipped for having a flawed style all of their own.

In retirement and through remembrance, deification is assured. When heroes are recalled, eyes moisten and those posters feel near again, as if you could walk through a door and back into the bedroom of your youth.

There is warmth in remembering football gone by. It opens the same chamber of the brain as memories of childhood homes and ice-cream vans. That is a comforting thing to hold onto.

ACKNOWLEDGEMENTS

For taking me in the first place, Dad; for always indulging and supporting me, Mum; for putting up with losing-weekend moods, Marisa; for making football sparkle anew, Kaitlyn. Heartfelt thanks to my agent David Luxton, my publisher Charlotte Croft, my editors Holly Jarrald and Sarah Connelly, and my copy-editor Karen Rigden.